D1630700

BIBLE TO GO!

Reading the Bible in everyday places

Sister Elizabeth Pio

First published in Great Britain in 2014

Society for Promoting Christian Knowledge
36 Causton Street
London SW1P 4ST
www.spckpublishing.co.uk

British Library Cataloguing-in-Publication Data
A catalogue record for this book is available from the British Library

ISBN 978–0–281–07123–4
eBook ISBN 978–0–281–07124–1

Typeset by Graphicraft Limited, Hong Kong
Manufacture managed by Jellyfish
First printed in Great Britain by CPI Group
Subsequently digitally printed in Great Britain

eBook by Graphicraft Limited, Hong Kong

Produced on paper from sustainable forests

Contents

Contents

Acknowledgements

Thank you to God for encouraging me to write this book and for giving me the outline for it during a 6 a.m. meditation session on a dark, chilly January day in 2013. Thank you to Lauren Zimmerman at SPCK for kicking all this off! Thanks to Mum for having the courage to walk into a pub with a nun and trying to look 'normal', while the aforementioned nun proceeds to meditate on the Bible over a bowl of ketchup-covered chips. Thank you to my Revd Mother, Rita-Elizabeth, for allowing me to undertake this project, for trawling through each chapter (sometimes in a bemused state), for her prayers, and for those of my Sisters. Last but not least, thank you to my beloved best friend Lil, a Parsons Jack Russell terrier, who fills my heart with joy, unconditional love and accepts me as I am (is it any coincidence that 'dog' and 'God' are so alike?).

For God,
who loves you as you are,
wherever you are

Nun in a pub (rare)

Imagine: you stroll into your local one evening and spot me at the bar, sipping an OJ, meditating on a packet of dry roasted.

YOU: Er, hello, Sister. What are you doing here?

ME: What are *you* doing here?!

YOU: Oh, I've just come from a friend's. *(Awkward silence, shifting of eyes)* Actually I was supposed to be reading my Bible and ... *(Tip: nuns can spot dishonesty a mile off; you might as well just confess!)*

ME: What's your poison?

YOU: . . . . *(Name your fave drink)*

ME: So, Bible reading's boring, huh?

YOU: Um ... yes.

ME: *(I beckon you to lean closer and whisper ...)* Table at 9 o'clock. See the vicar? She's talking about you.

YOU: Me?!!

ME: Yep.

YOU: What's she saying? How do you know she's ...?

ME: We eat in silence; I can lip read.

YOU: Wow! Well? Come on: tell me what she's saying.

ME: See how keen you are to know? Do you know that every time you read your Bible you give God a chance to talk, to tell you something about yourself, your life, work, love, anything? Don't miss out, comrade. Be as keen to hear what *he*'s saying.

YOU: I hadn't seen it like that before.

ME: So we're going to meet every week to hear what he has to say to you, OK? See you in Costa, bring your Bible.

YOU: Costa? Hang on, Sister! What was the vicar saying about me?

ME: That Edna and the girls love you and have co-opted you on to the flower rota. Please don't ask me to help; I can't tell an agapanthus from a Stradivarius. Ciao, God bless!

But before we get to Costa . . .

. . . a word in your shell-like. Why should you bother reading on? If, as I said in the pub, you want to hear God and to deepen your relationship with him (or her) through reading your Bible. This is neither a Bible study guide nor a commentary but more like – to give it a hip name – 'urban lectio divina'. It's about reading the Bible prayerfully but in an everyday urban setting, allowing God to speak to you through his word and through where you are. What, even in Costa?

Yes, even in Costa – that's our first port of call. The ninth-century teacher Eriugena taught that the living word of God could be found by reading two books: first, the 'small' book, the Bible; second, the 'big' book (which can't be bought from Amazon), creation. So that's what we're going to do. We're going to read our Bibles in 20 'everyday' places, soaking up God's word and creation. Our Bibles *deserve* to be read wherever we are; it's where they belong. HP printers have a User Manual; we have a Life Manual – the Bible – so use it. Now if you're thinking, 'There's no way I'm walking into a coffee shop with my dusty, black, dog-eared King James Version', then listen up. Grab yourself a version you're comfy with – if you don't do 'art' and 'thou', don't be a prune (massive respect to those fruits whether in syrup or juice): get a modern one with a flashy cover. Some Bibles even look like clutch bags and Filofaxes, so there's no damage to your street cred, diggit? Aside from that, nobody can see what you're reading on your tablet.

Too many of us separate our church life from the rest of our life. It's my prayer that through reading this book your life won't be separated in this way – that's not how it was meant to be. God made everything. He's in all things. Everyone is made in the image of God, whether or not they're religious. God is everywhere, not just in a church or rectory. Therefore all people and all places have a 'sacredness' – yes, even a pub. (That doesn't mean I'm excusing those who regularly sink ten pints and enjoy starting punch-ups over the pool table. A pub's a great place to be with friends and family. It's all down to how we use a place.) So all creation – people, places, material things – bear the footprints of their Maker.

I can feel my gingerbread latte calling so, lastly, throughout our travels we'll be using 'GRAB' (Go! Relax, Absorb, Bible time) – the most up-to-date, state of the art, eco-friendly Bible reading system in the world, developed in conjunction with TEA (Theological Education Authority) and CAKE (Christian Academy of Knowledge and Ethics):

Go! Visit all 20 places if you can (four of them are actually television programmes). If you can't then I'll help you use a gift God has given you – your imagination.

Relax When you get to a place *stop*, sit down and chill out. God's Spirit can find it hard to get through to you if you're all tensed up. I'll give you a very short prayer to use to ask God for his help. It's important to invite him in to what you're about to do – you can't do it without him.

Absorb the place you're in. Most of us, even nuns, tend to go from one place or activity to the next without taking *any* notice of where we are. So let your soul catch up with the rest of you. Spend time taking a good look around, making it your own, becoming a part of the scene. What do you hear, smell, touch and see? God is there, this is his creation, so *read* it because he can speak to you through your senses. Before you even pick up your Bible or this book, you might find a certain smell strikes a chord, reminding you out of the blue of some past event. Do you feel drawn to stick with that? If you do, *don't stuff it away in your mind like a pair of embarrassing underpants!* This could be the Holy Spirit nudging you to bring it to God, so dwell on it in his presence and let him speak to you. Put down your Bible, or this book, and stay with what you're feeling, because God's leading you into prayer.

Bible time We'll read a Bible passage slowly, more than once. I'll then pick up on a word, a phrase or the gist of what's going on and give you something to think and talk with God about in the context of where you are. *Warning:* you may find another word or phrase leaping out at you – this, again, could be the Holy Spirit nudging you, so stay with that word and come back to the book another time.

All Bible passages were chosen at random. I simply went to the car boot sale or the football match, opened my Bible and absorbed the first chunk of text I saw. After re-reading two or three times, the subject matter for each chapter emerged. This is an example of the Holy Spirit at work – I didn't choose the topics for this book, *he* did. You can do the same, so have a go yourself: take your Bible with you to work, for example; do as I did and let God's Spirit speak to *you*.

By the way, along with my Bible, most of the time I'll be bringing my best friend. She's a fruity Parsons Jack Russell called Lil – beard, bushy eyebrows and burps after every meal.

Now, have you ordered your 'Bible to go'? OK, time for a gingerbread latte to drink in. Woohoo!

1

Go! God makes the difference in Costa

————•◦•————

☺ RELAX

Father God, this is life and you are here. Speak to me through
what I read, see, smell and touch. In Jesus' name. Amen.

☺ ABSORB

We find ourselves a quiet table and sink into luxurious leather-
effect armchairs that instantly make you wonder how many
attempts you'll need to get up and out. Relax. Lil isn't with
us today; she's visiting the mobile grooming parlour to have
her beard, eyebrows and coat trimmed, and her nails seen
to (she can resemble some kind of miniature warthog otherwise). Mmm: the aroma of mocha Italia! The bang, grind
and frothing of the machines. Are they real plants, do you
think? Smiley baristas with spiky hair. Biscotti. Someone's
wearing Chanel No. 5. The quiet buzz of conversation.
Occasional laughter. What colour are the walls? Trendy chalkboards. What is that a picture of? An Italian back street,
I think, in greyscale on a huge canvas. The lighting's very . . .
mmm . . . intimate and IKEA. A discarded newspaper on a
table. A student's immersed in her smartphone. Lots of dark

work surfaces. Huge pictures of coffee cups. Two young mums chat while their toddlers busy themselves eating napkins. A queue's building because everyone's asking for the seasonal special, which takes ages to make. This table's a bit wonky. Subtle background R&B. My gingerbread latte stands proud in a tall glass with a handle that's really low down. That first sip . . . mmm . . . the taste! A momentary milk moustache accompanies a heavenly blend of bitter sweetness. How's yours? What did you order? I don't know about you but I feel I could drop off; it's warm, comfy and somehow feels like home. You know, I don't think those plants are real, they're too . . . shiny.

YOU: Don't you feel embarrassed walking into a coffee shop, Sister?

ME: What, with you? No! Don't put yourself down! You want to watch that: it could be the beginning of some kind of inferiority complex. Now, come on: I hear the lattes calling!

YOU: No, I meant . . .

When you're ready, it's . . .

✍ BIBLE TIME

Let's read Mark 9.38–41.

'Teacher,' said John, 'we saw someone driving out demons in your name and we told him to stop, because he was not one of us.' 'Do not stop him,' Jesus said. 'For no one who does a miracle in my name can in the next moment say anything bad about me, for whoever is not against us is for us. Truly I tell you, anyone who gives you a cup of water in my name because you belong to the Messiah will certainly not lose their reward.'

Read it through again.

So what's God saying?

The words 'not one of us' stand out. The apostles seem to be saying, 'That bloke's not one of us so he's wrong'! Jesus doesn't think so. How do you feel towards people who think differently from you, who have different opinions from you? What's your attitude to difference? God might be encouraging you to explore that with him.

God didn't make us all the same. Oh no: we're made to measure. Let's look around – we're surrounded by difference. Some of our 'Costa cousins' love lattes but detest espressos. Some may be Beliebers while others may adore Engelbert Humperdinck. Some may be Christians, others will have no time for religion. Notice the different fashions – the student wearing combats and classic Nikes, the mums' chinos and UGG boots, the street surfer with blonde highlights and Billabong (by the way, when it comes to fashion I'm keeping silent). Some of us prefer Twitter to Facebook. We get on better with some people than with others, don't we? Would you enjoy a frappuccino opposite someone enthusiastically informing you of what Klingons eat for breakfast? Or perhaps you'd prefer a mocha with Donna who loves to give you – or actually anyone – constant updates on her bowel movements? So there we have it, we simply *have* to live with difference, and most of the time we can all live pretty peacefully with differences like these. However, what about the things that really get up our noses, that affect our lives, make us angry and cause us to argue in our families, at work, in our churches? Mmm . . . I think it's time to play 'P-p-p-pick on a person' . . .

Pick a person in this coffee shop, someone who catches your eye. Now, if the two of you got to know each other I'm pretty sure that, eventually, you'd discover a major 'difference' – you don't agree on women being bishops or you support different political parties perhaps. You could back off and stop talking to one another; after all, your relationship's never going to be the same now, is it? What if you had to live or work together? Constantly avoiding someone takes a lot of effort and can cause us mega loads of stress. It makes us feel uneasy, doesn't it? We don't actually like it. Why? It goes against the human condition. God made us to be social animals to enjoy sweet fellowship with others. So what do we do? I think I can see some clues . . .

For some perverse reason, when I think of sweet fellowship I think of that comedy *The Royle Family*. Jim and Barb are the patriarchal and matriarchal figures in the cast and they're very different. Barb screws up her face in disgust every time Jim picks his nose and wipes the results on his shirt, or boasts about his exploits in the toilet. There's a clue there – really, there is.

I see Manchester City have made the headlines on that discarded copy of *The Times* over there. I remember City boss Roberto Mancini forever clashing heads with striker Mario Balotelli – two very different characters, of different generations, one of them in a position of authority. Their difference affected other players and became increasingly disruptive. There's another clue there – honest, I'm a nun.

Barb loves Jim simply for who he is. The godliness of love makes anything bearable – yes, even string vests and sweaty armpits. Mancini proclaimed that he would forgive Balotelli time and time again because he could see his potential (doesn't that sound like something Jesus said?). So what's the clue as to what we should do? *Relationship.* We need to try to form a relationship with those who are different. We can choose to walk away, to avoid them, but we'll be getting on the motorway to nowhere. It's true that those people we find most difficult to get on with are often the ones who are actually able to help us grow the most. Doh! How annoying.

So difference can be an invitation to relationship. Building a relationship with someone who gets on your wick isn't easy though, is it, so how do we do it? Well, it's not easy, but here we go:

1 Grab a coffee.
2 Remember that we're all equally valued and loved by God.
3 Remember that we're not God; we don't have a monopoly on the truth; we're not always right; we should keep an open mind with the intention of listening and learning.
4 *Listen* to the other person. Don't interrupt her (or him). You'll find yourself meeting the 'person' behind the opinion. We're all products of our past, so where's that person who's getting your back up coming from? Why does she view something so differently from me? Perhaps if you'd had her past you'd agree with her! Listen in order to learn and understand. Because you've listened to her, she (or he) is more likely to listen to you.

5 Be prepared to change your opinion if you feel it's right to (you won't always). Don't be afraid. Ditch your pride. Your opinion should never be your god – God should be.

So relationship's important. Perhaps difference is an invitation to *come together* rather than back off. When we stop talking our imagination goes into overdrive and we build up illusions and resentments about others. God made us all differently and he also told us to love our 'enemy'. Those who are 'not one of us' can be seen as our enemies. So love them by listening. Is there someone you need to be listening to?

ME: Right, I'm off. *Don't* forget to use your long spoon to scoop up the foam after you've finished; it's unforgivable if you don't – only kidding. Lil and I will meet you next in Sainsbury's car park, on the bench in front of that huge sign saying 'Live well for less'. And don't forget: *thank* God for this time. Arrivederci. God bless!

2

Go! God's greatest in Sainsbury's car park

———•◦•———

☺ RELAX

My God, this is life and you are here. Where I am, you are. Open my heart as I listen for your voice. In Jesus' name. Amen.

☺ ABSORB

We've found ourselves a quiet bench. Clashing trolleys. The distant *beep-beep* of a cash point. A Ford Fiesta cruises the wrong way in the one-way system, the driver battling to open a packet of Jammie Dodgers. Trolley queues of enormous length being pushed effortlessly by attendants. A car hand-wash gang loiters. Is that a plane flying somewhere above the clouds? Little old ladies joke with their taxi-drivers. Post-shoppers huddle satisfactorily in their cars scoffing treats as though they haven't seen food for weeks. What's the weather like? Is that rain? Pre-shoppers roam searching for the right shape trolley. Lone staff mill outside smoking. Lil's sniffing the air because a businessman's about to eat a car lunch of freshly cooked chicken from the deli. A woman fights with a rebellious trolley that's determined to go its own way – check out her radioactive green mini-skirt! We must be sitting near the restaurant – I'm sure I can smell chips. Someone can't be bothered to return his trolley so leaves it stranded to take up a parking space. Is it warm out here? This bench is cold to the touch; I hope we don't get piles. A slight breeze rustles leaves and powers straying carrier bags. I'm not sure that space is big enough for the person who's trying, for the tenth time, to reverse into it. The boot's going to be awkward for them to get to when they come back – should we tell them?! Too late: they're in. While we've been engrossed Lil's nicked a packet of liquorice allsorts from our carrier bag. A solid liquorice Bertie Bassett is stretching between her chomping jaws like an elastic band. On that note . . . to your surprise I reveal an iPad displaying today's Bible text.

YOU: Sister! I thought you'd taken a vow of poverty.
ME: I have. It's been lent to me, so there. It's an illusion
       that the only tablets nuns know about are those
       they get on prescription.

When you're ready, it's . . .

✎ BIBLE TIME

Let's read Mark 9.33–35.

> They came to Capernaum. When he was in the house, he asked them, 'What were you arguing about on the road?' But they kept quiet because on the way they had argued about who was the greatest. Sitting down, Jesus called the Twelve and said, 'Anyone who wants to be first must be the very last, and the servant of all.'

Read it through again.

So what's God saying?

I don't know about you but my life's been littered with 'Who's the greatest?' competitions, from 'I bet my fingers can be bent back further than yours without me screaming', to contests of who can gorge the most chocolates without being sick (we Sisters really should grow up – only kidding: such rivalries are from my previous life). So here the apostles have had a conflab about who's the greatest and have walked right into a new definition. Does God want to share that definition with you too?

Which of these people working for Sainsbury's could be described as the 'greatest'? If greatness is measured by how much power or authority a person has, surely the store manager's the greatest. If greatness is measured by how much a person earns, maybe it's the shopper who can buy Taste the Difference products and then load them into the boot of a Merc. Lots of us measure greatness like that. But God doesn't.

God measures greatness very differently. He sees greatness in people who look to use their God-given gifts and talents for others rather than to benefit themselves. Great people wonder how they can help God's world rather than how they can eat out more in higher class restaurants.

So who's the greatest in this store? It could be Dave on the checkout, Leanne who's stacking shelves or Brian overlooking finances. It could be Ian the store manager and it could even be Eileen with her Merc. We can't tell. Only God knows. We must be careful not to judge.

There's a 'rightness' that's felt in caring for others, isn't there? It feels good when you know you're benefiting someone else, as though it's a natural human thing to do, as though we were made for others. We get so much back too – in giving we also receive. Supermarket staff can be so helpful, packing bags, helping the elderly with their money, bearing up with those of us who want to buy a packet of fig rolls with a voucher for Pedigree Chum. When we simply look out for ourselves we turn inward, ignoring the needs of others, and wonder why we don't have the relationships we deeply crave. That's not what God wants for me or you.

Who's the greatest – Phil, Éric, Lance or Linda? Hard man Phil Mitchell in *EastEnders*, with his swagger, scowl, permanently furrowed brow and heavy breathing, is always interested in making a mint for himself. He wants to be the greatest, to have power and influence, to own property, to cruise his Jag around the Square (he melts when he's at family dos in the Vic though . . . before the inevitable punch-up of course).

Barcelona defender Éric Abidal underwent a liver transplant in April 2012. This naturally threatened his future playing career. However, rather than push himself he decided not to take any chances. His family took priority over any future glory; if he couldn't play then he'd be with his loved ones. Top man.

Gifted cyclist Lance Armstrong won seven Tour de France races – amazing. However, in January 2013 he admitted to taking illegal performance-enhancing drugs during all seven wins, and was stripped of all his titles. He so wanted to be the greatest, to be a god.

Through my cell wall I can hear Linda, a carer, visiting our eldest Sister. The loving way she talks and tends to her never ceases to astound me considering her tight schedule and the nature of her work.

Whether they know it or not, Éric and Linda are walking in the way of their Maker. God is there too for 'Phil' and Lance, loving them gently to greatness beyond their wildest dreams.

So do *you* want to be the greatest? There's nothing wrong with that ambition, but what's your motive: helping yourself to greatness or helping others? Be brutally honest – this can all be very subtle. In my former life as a marketing manager I was raking it in for myself. I wanted to fill my trolley with expensive coffee and luxury ice-cream. My work was everything; family and friends had to take second place. I would set my sights on sales figures like a 'heat-seeking missile in heels' (from one of Victoria Wood's delightful phrases). Now I have no money but am so much richer by helping others. Have a think.

ME: Right: come on, Lil: a generous smothering of barbecue-beef-flavour toothpaste for you, I think. We'll see you next at the train station, Platform 1. By the coffee shop, naturally. Enjoy your time with God. Bon soir! Oh, and don't forget to *thank* God! Bye!

3

Go! Judging Judy at the train station

☺ RELAX

Father God, this is life and you are here. Enfold me, teach
me, speak to my heart. In Jesus' name. Amen.

☺ ABSORB

We're sitting in the shade of Platform 1 of the train station,
that curiously romantic place of tearful farewells and good
riddances. Both Lil and I have made an effort to blend
in – I'm donning a pair of Dr Dre wireless headphones and
Lil's tweeting on her iBone. Yeah man, we're connected.
There's a buzz of conversation. Anxious looks at departure
screens. Someone's lost his temper and is having a go at the
poor girl trying to serve lattes. The whistle of the guard –
it's rather archaic, shouldn't he be tweeting instead? The
chug of a waiting train. Surprisingly clear announcements.
Bored children, tired of the novelty of a day out on the
train. Laughter. Coffee. Someone's wearing Clinique 'Happy'.
A 'train wash', hoardings – why are station surroundings
so depressing? Flowery shorts highlight a tourist. Cyclists.
Rucksacks. Satchels. Timetables. Ringtones. 'Is this the train
for Derby?' 'No, Madam, it's a luggage trolley.' Briefcases. Hey,
someone's got a text message! Toilets, passenger assistance.

Mmm . . . that smell of not-quite-Costa cappuccinos. Suits, jeans, red hair, no hair. A billboard promoting air travel (is it cheaper than rail?). The obligatory graffiti. Expensive sarnies. WHSmith. Kindles. People rushing to make connections, screaming kids.

YOU: Do you ever regret not having had children, Sister?

ME: No. God gave me a Parsons Jack Russell instead. She never throws tantrums in public, burps herself, and will never need help with maths homework. She ticks all the boxes.

Nobody bats an eyelid as we get out our tablets. When you're ready, it's . . .

☞ BIBLE TIME

Let's read Romans 2.1–4.

> You, therefore, have no excuse, you who pass judgment on someone else, for at whatever point you judge another, you are condemning yourself, because you who pass judgment do the same things. Now we know that God's judgment against those who do such things is based on truth. So when you, a mere human being, pass judgment on them and yet do the same things, do you think you will escape God's judgment? Or do you show contempt for the riches of his kindness, forbearance and patience, not realising that God's kindness is intended to lead you to repentance?

Read it through again.

So what's God saying?

One of my main preoccupations at a train station is to 'people watch'. I can have someone's life mapped out in five minutes – can you? As we read this Bible passage I feel God's saying something like, 'Are you "people watching" or "people judging"?' Mmm . . . I'm judging. I've been judging for so long I don't realize I'm doing it! Are you like that too? Yes? Take a seat and we'll perform an exercise (no leotard required). You're not like that? Sit down anyway, although I wouldn't want to get you into bad habits – bad 'habits', get it? No . . .

There's an announcement – 'The person now arriving on Platform 1 is Judy.' OK, here's Judy, the person we're going to perform our exercise on. So the first stage of 'people watching' is to watch. Now, I would guess Judy's about 5ft 5in., she's plump, mid-forties, do you think? White. She's wearing a neat 'forensic gown blue' suit, with a skirt, but it looks fairly cheap. Short hair, browny blonde, dyed, possibly covering grey. Deep red lipstick, light blue eye shadow, mascara, foundation with blusher. She's wearing gold rings, gold sleeper ear-rings and a chunky turquoise necklace. Shoes are low heel, a navy blue. Tights are a natural shade. Perfume's heavy, possibly Dior 'Poison'? A bulky, black leather case with a broken flap that's seen better days. Judy's looking quite at ease; she must be a seasoned train user, a commuter perhaps? Uh-oh, she's looking over here, at us.

JUDY: Oh, there's a nun. Wonder what she's doing here. Probably going to a church fete somewhere to help run a bric-a-brac stall. She can't be going home, they don't do that, do they? I hope Catherine doesn't decide to waste her life like that – over my dead body. Nobody in their right mind would want to cut themselves off from the world like that. Weird.

ME: She must be a regular traveller, yes? Middle management perhaps? Frustrated at not making the leap to director level; she's had to cover the grey. Yes, her body shape says she's clearly put business first in life; there's been no time for exercise but plenty of opportunity to indulge in business brunches. Mmm . . . she's married, but I bet hubby's fed up with her hours and microwaved Spag bol with wine every night.

JUDY: I wonder if she gets fed up wearing the same old thing every day. What an absolute nightmare; I couldn't stand that. And no hair? I remember that film I saw once, the wind blew a nun's veil off and she had a crew cut, a crew cut! I expect she's got long johns on underneath, woolly ones from the 1950s. Why on earth would someone want to do that? Ugh! No perfume, no make-up. No sex – no way.

ME: Looks as though Judy's still got a point to prove in life. She desperately wants to make her mark, and now she's reached her mid-forties she's going for it with high impact make-up and jewellery – there's to be no second chances. Children, mmm . . . probably not doing very well at school because of their troubled parents; too much of a burden for dad. The house is pretty empty most of the time, what do you reckon? Judy's normally in the office-cum-spare-bedroom-cum-ironing-board room. Most of the household items are on hire purchase.

JUDY: I bet she was brought up reading prayer books. Must be pretty holy by now. Doesn't she ever get bored? I wonder what she does for fun? Probably doesn't have any – they did in *Sister Act* though. She's got headphones on. Must be listening to some churchy choir; it's not likely to be Iron Maiden, is it? Ha, ha! Genesis, maybe? Tee-hee.

ME: They go to Spain or Cornwall every year, but she takes her laptop and checks her emails while hubby's driving the barbecue. She's got a company car, probably a red Renault Scenic. Does her main shop at Asda – that's where she got that suit from. Hang on; she's going. Her train's in. Exercise complete.

GOD: Not quite, Sister.

ME: Oh, hello God.

GOD: Let's look at that Bible passage from Romans again – 'at whatever point you judge another, you are condemning yourself, because you who pass judgment do the same things.' Did your judgement of Judy reflect anything about your own life?

ME: Um . . . let me think now . . . um, yes . . . I suppose it did. Mmm . . . yes, I hadn't realized that actually. There are similarities, I suppose. Trying to climb the career ladder, putting the job over people, a craving for some kind of success; yes, OK: I'm beginning to see some things.

GOD: You labelled Judy with all manner of things that actually apply to you. Do you feel better about yourself, that you've made yourself 'superior' to someone?

ME: Yes . . . I admit I suppose I did feel pretty good creating a problematic life for someone else.

GOD: Only my judgement is based on truth. I know Judy best, as I know you too. You create illusions that harm your own soul. You will carry these judgements and reapply them to other people. Your preconceived ideas will end up harming your relationships.

ME: Sorry. Will you help me not to do that again?

GOD: Of course I will, but be patient with yourself. You'll do it again and again, but we'll work together until, one day, you'll realize you're not doing it any more. By the way, Judy's 52, happily married, with children at university, and is patron of an international children's charity. You were right about the Scenic and Cornwall though.

ME: Wow – thank you.

GOD: She thought you were wasting your life, had no hair, wore woolly long johns, were prayer-book savvy, mega holy, had no fun and liked churchy music.

ME: What?! How wrong could she be?!

GOD: Exactly.

ME: Phew, there's nothing like learning from God! I could do with a latte, even though it's not Costa. Are you coming? Lil can nibble a biscotti while she tweets. Where are we meeting next? In front of the telly for *EastEnders*? I've always felt Dirty Den was judged unfairly, that he was a diamond geezer really. See you soon, Alfie Moon!

4

Go! Meeting God in Albert Square

☺ RELAX

Father God, this is life and you are here. Bless us with your presence as we read your holy word. In Jesus' name. Amen.

☺ ABSORB

We're making ourselves comfortable in front of the telly as that familiar intro to *EastEnders* begins. Lil, observing my 'no play' look, drops her tennis ball and curls up between us sighing heavily (the sign of contentment or the acceptance of boredom?).

YOU: Do you miss watching telly, Sister?
ME: No – but I do enjoy the occasional episode of *Dog the Bounty Hunter*. I like his hair, and their prayer circles are superb.

Let's watch two or three scenes of *EastEnders* to get the feel of it. Warning: try not to get caught up in the story; distance yourself and simply look at what's in each scene. If you're an avid fan then watch the episode beforehand. Why is this soap so dark? Even in the daytime it's gloomy. What's in the background? Are we in the café, the Queen Vic? Note the lighting, the mood of the scene. What are people wearing?

There appears to be a dress code for the men of dark leather jackets, dark jeans and dark boots. What time of day is it? After a few minutes we turn the volume right down and continue watching. Note the different facial expressions and body language. Some scenes will be heavy with emotion – stress, tension, furrowed brows, violence, anger, red faces, worry or tears. Some – not many – will be full of joy, laughter, love, happiness or peace. Take a look at any artwork or paintings . . . or tattoos; any pictures on walls, ornaments. What's the decor like? What's being sold in the market today? Can you see any posters promoting local events, any billboards? Notice hairstyles, make-up, the general look of each character.

OK, when you're ready, it's . . .

✎ BIBLE TIME

Let's read Job 40.1–14.

The LORD said to Job: 'Will the one who contends with the Almighty correct him? Let him who accuses God answer him!' Then Job answered the LORD: 'I am unworthy – how can I reply to you? I put my hand over my mouth. I spoke once, but I have no answer – twice, but I will say no more.' Then the LORD spoke to Job out of the storm: 'Brace yourself like a man; I will question you, and you shall answer me. Would you discredit my justice? Would you condemn me to justify yourself? Do you have an arm like God's, and can your voice thunder like his? Then adorn yourself with glory and splendour, and clothe yourself in honour and majesty. Unleash the fury of your wrath, look at all who are proud and bring them low, look at all who are proud and humble them, crush the wicked where they stand. Bury them all in the dust together; shroud their faces in the grave. Then I myself will admit to you that your own right hand can save you.'

Read it through again.

So what's God saying?

In this passage Job is meeting with God. After around 30 chapters of Job lamenting and listening to his friends, God enters the scene and changes the direction of the book. It's a powerful meeting where the Source of all puts Job in his place, ending the laments and asserting his authority. As a result Job is changed at a very deep level. Perhaps God wants to meet with *you* . . . more often?

When we meet with God we change, sometimes instantly, sometimes over time – if you're mathematical, YOU + GOD = YOU CHANGE. We cannot meet with God and remain the same. That can be very uncomfortable because we may think we're 'all right'. We may need to believe more, feel the need to go to church more – but not to CHANGE?! Job found out how uncomfortable meeting with God can be.

EastEnders is a series of meetings; seldom is someone alone in a scene. Did you notice reactions as people met with each other? Some warmed to meeting a particular person while some were clearly on the defensive. Body language, expression and general attitude depended on who the character was with and the relationship with that person. How do you feel when you meet with God? Do you look forward to times with him? Do you find them boring? Perhaps you resent feeling as though you have to come away from usual activities; to get prayer time over and done with in order to move on guilt-free to something more interesting? Be honest.

Who are you when you meet with God? Jack in *EastEnders* is much more relaxed in his body, face and mannerisms and displays an attitude of wanting to please when he's with a 'bird'. However, bring on Phil Mitchell and he turns into a tense, aggressive Rottweiler (oops – sorry Lil). When I'm with my family I'm the daughter or sister with a long history of BMX racing, of hiding behind the sofa from Daleks and impersonating the Incredible Hulk every time the show came on television. However, when I'm with my Sisters I'm a practical woman who loves trying to fix water pumps and knows her way around a smartphone. We can slip into certain roles depending on who we're with.

Are you 'yourself' with God? Kat Moon wears a lot of make-up. Fatboy dons colourful gear with a 'name'. Phil keeps his hair short. Max is seldom seen without his 'whistle and flute' (Cockney rhyming slang for 'suit'). I cover my head with a veil. What we wear gives out an image of who we are, but is it 'true'? Are we trying to cover up our real selves in order to present a popular and socially acceptable image? Perhaps we're simply trying to attract the attention of others. Is it an effort or a chore to present ourselves in a certain way, or are we comfortable with it? There was a time I wouldn't be seen dead without make-up – I couldn't let certain people see what I *really* looked like! Now, I honestly don't care because I'm secure in God's love and in the love that others have for me, and I'm certainly not trying to attract anyone! Do you feel you need to prepare and then present yourself in a certain way before you meet with God?

What about attitude? When Masood is with Ayesha he gives her his full attention; his eyes sparkle because she's of interest to him and can give him something he wants. He's different with Carol; he has no need of anything from her, perhaps not even friendship, and so directs his attention elsewhere. Phil will suck up to the contact who can benefit him financially but the geezer without any influence might as well not exist. When you meet with God do you simply reel off a list of 'wants'? Or don't you ask for anything at all? Do you see him as a 'cosmic cash machine'? Perhaps approaching him in times of need is easy, but when everything's hunky-dory you don't need to bother him.

So what about meeting God? Wouldn't it be funny if the characters in *EastEnders* began meeting with God?

MAX: 'Ere, Sharon, where's Phil? The garage is all locked up.
SHARON: He's gone on retreat with the Sisters of summink; he'll be back in a week.

Or:

ALFIE: Look Rox, I'm dying to be alone wiv' yer. 'Ow abaht we meet outside the Vic at 8?
ROXY: Sorry, Alfie; I'll be prayin' me rosary then.

Entire books have been written on meeting with God, but let's address a few things. God longs for you to spend time with him. Knowing that is important. There's nothing worse than feeling as though you're wasting time. He's there and he listens.

'God time' shouldn't always feel like a chore (sometimes it will!). You are giving him a chance to speak with you. It's a bit like having a telephone conversation – you remain silent while you listen to the person on the other end. Hand him the phone and listen up.

Be yourself with God. If you're fed up and can't be bothered to give God time, go somewhere on your own and tell him what's bothering you. He's not expecting prayer formulas; he wants YOU, so let him have it! Anything else is 'ou' of order, d'ya 'ear me?'

Don't copy someone else's devotion. We're called to spend time with God in different ways. How you spend time with God during your life will change. I could imagine Dot Branning reciting the Divine Mercy Chaplet, while Ian Beale might be drawn to meditating on kitchen utensils. Staying close to God is the aim.

ME: Come on, Lil – we're off. We'll see you next in the precinct on the bench outside Claire's. Don't sit there all night munching Pringles. And don't forget to you-know-what. Gotta go – Lil's dying for a Dairylea. Ta-ra!

5

Go! God's for all in the shopping mall!

☺ RELAX

Jesus, this is life and you are here. Speak to me through my
senses, open my heart to hear you. Amen.

☺ ABSORB

We find a bench without chewing gum by the raised flower
beds. Concrete and pigeons – there's lots of both. The birds
strut then stop, staring into our eyes, waiting for a Gregg's
sausage roll. They're quite intimidating – not the sausage
rolls, the birds – they're bullying us! Then Lil emerges from
behind the skirt of my habit and in the quiver of a whiskery
dog's beard . . . they're gone! There's a faint whiff of espresso.
Someone's smoking. Distant traffic. Clinton Cards. Card
Factory. Hot sandwiches. An elderly couple discuss benefit
cuts and varicose vein stripping. The click, click, click of high
heels. Babies gurgling a conversation. Laughter – a smoker's
laugh. A dormant merry-go-round. Pushchairs that resemble
miniature mobile homes. There's up to 75 per cent off in
Claire's. Nobody's in Specsavers – I suppose they couldn't
find it. Smartphones. The *beep-beep-beep* of a cash machine.

It's overcast, and I must say this bench is pretty hard; wished we'd chosen one with chewing gum on now. A young family scoff rolls and coffee from Gregg's. A gaggle of girls share their views on glow-in-the-dark bikinis. A vacant-looking flower seller's outside WHSmith. A baby boy's screaming because Mum's gone to Iceland; he wanted to go to Pound Shop. Two girls – I think – wearing leather jackets and stripy tights giggle in our direction.

YOU: Tut – I think they're laughing at you, Sister. That's so unkind.

ME: Um – I don't think so. I'm afraid Lil's getting amorous with your left leg; that's probably what's entertaining them – naughty girl! It's corduroy: does it all the time.

When you're ready, it's . . .

☞ BIBLE TIME

Let's read 1 Timothy 2.1–7.

> I urge, then, first of all, that petitions, prayers, interces-sion and thanksgiving be made for all people – for kings and all those in authority, that we may live peaceful and quiet lives in all godliness and holiness. This is good, and pleases God our Saviour, who wants all people to be saved and to come to a knowledge of the truth. For there is one God and one mediator between God and mankind, the man Christ Jesus, who gave himself as a ransom for all people. This has now been witnessed to at the proper time. And for this purpose I was appointed

a herald and an apostle – I am telling the truth, I am not lying – and a true and faithful teacher of the Gentiles.

Read it through again.

So what's God saying?

God wants 'all people to be saved'. Jesus gave himself 'as a ransom for all people'. Not just me and you. Not just Christians. Not just people we like. He wants to be in the lives of those girls in stripy tights, that bloke with red hair and a nose ring, the bruiser whose cargo pants are hanging halfway down his legs (gosh, if you're looking for somewhere to park your bike then . . .). God is for everyone. Jesus is the Son of Man not the Son of Christians. He's for all. That's really, really good news, isn't it? There's a catch, though. These people need to know that God wants them. Perhaps he's suggesting that's where we come in.

We are his hands, his feet; we are his reps on earth. It's down to us to tell people about the love God has for them. So we'd better unpack our remote-controlled travelling soapbox, hadn't we? You do the talking and I'll operate the control box from that discreet alleyway over there. No? OK, we're not all called to spill words of wisdom in a shopping precinct. In fact having been an atheist for most of my life I can report that it can be the most ineffective form of evangelism – it's actually turned me away because I've found such speakers intrusive, annoying and irrelevant. What would have made an impact is noticing how someone lived her life. 'She's different, somehow. Why?' 'Why does he seem to have a peace about him even when the computer's crashed and the baby's vomited in his ear?' 'How come they don't gossip or say anything nasty about anyone?' They're different. Perhaps we *can* evangelize in this place . . .

Madge is in the precinct – how can we tell her about God? She's over the moon with her blue rinse. She can't stop because she *has* to be home by three, sitting comfortably in front of the telly, crumpet on one side, Yorkshire tea on the other, to watch *Dickinson's Real Deal*. Plus she thinks Christians are a load of hypocrites. However, she just has time to pop into Oxfam to see if there's a sale. Madge has spotted an apostle spoon set at half price . . . but it's on the top shelf. She can't get it – but you can. You pass her the bargain with a smile; you might even whisper, 'God bless'. Pray for God's blessing upon her and leave the rest up to him.

Jay's been working on the till at Superdrug for three years, engaged to Kaylee-Ann but in love with Lady Gaga. He survives on Pot Noodles and Pop-Tarts and can't wait until 1 o'clock to have a smoke and tweet. 'Hi, how are you?' you ask as you pass Jay your corn plasters. 'Yeah, bonza, thanks. Be even better in a coupla' hours' ('nice of 'em to ask', he thinks). Pray that God will bless Jay today.

'Angel' has escaped from the building site for half an hour to buy a birthday prezzie for the missus from Pound Shop (his mates call him Angel because of his 'wings' – the flabby bits men are prone to develop on their waists as they journey through life). After selecting a deluxe, gift-wrapped box of broken biscuits he can't ignore a bag of stink bombs, a grow-your-own Venus flytrap kit, two whoopee cushions and an inflatable Mr Blobby for the kids. As you're queuing with your dual-function swede masher/fly swatter you spot Angel behind you. Seeing his hands so full you invite him to go before you. He's surprised and grateful. Ask God to make himself known to Angel.

Fresh from the spa, Diana loves to browse in Edinburgh Woollen Mill, conveniently located on the edge of the precinct so she doesn't have to venture too near the masses. As she approaches the store she passes you and you throw her a smile and a 'Good morning'. 'A smile?' thinks Diana, 'a smile?! They smiled at me. No one smiles – it may mean a reapplication of a very expensive foundation. How can they smile? They don't have an Aga and ten acres, so how can they?' Ask God to bless Diana today.

Evangelism? These are just good deeds – everyone can do them, can't they? True, everyone can do them, but they don't. And not everyone prays. Never underestimate the power and capability of God to make himself known to someone. Remember that we're not expected to do all the work ourselves – we're in partnership with him. Let God provide the sunshine on the little seeds we sow (someone else may be in charge of the watering can). We may think we haven't made any impact whatsoever on a person. We may be right – but we may be wrong. I'm constantly amazed at the seemingly insignificant things people remember that have lingered in their hearts and made a big difference to their lives. Only God can see what's happening in a person's soul. A kind deed and a prayer – two gifts to make anyone feel valued. God is certainly for all in this shopping precinct.

ME: Right, Lil, come with me – leave that leg alone! A visit to Bob's Bathrooms, I think, to get her a cold shower. Oh, hang on – we're in the bathroom next. Perhaps she can loofah in there. Woohoo! Be there or be square! Arrivederci!

6

Go! Scrubbing up with God in the bathroom

☺ RELAX

Father God, this is life and you are here. I give this time to you. I lift up my worries. Open my heart to receive your word and your peace. In Jesus' name. Amen.

☉ ABSORB

Now, before we make ourselves comfortable I feel duty bound to say that this is *Bible* time. If you need to perform a particular function in this room, get it over and done with before we begin.

Aah, bathrooms tend to be so peaceful. Calming colours (normally), frayed toothbrushes, topless deodorants, manky showerheads, hairy soap, shower gels parading in pairs as a result of BOGOF offers, toilet rolls waiting either on a hoop-la stick or in a bread basket, mmm . . . someone's trying the Lynx effect . . . it's not working, scrunchies hanging up since Christmas . . . 2006, mildew, Mr Muscle, bottles of non-drip shower gels that have been closed just in case. Oh no! Lil's found a pair of dusty underpants that have been lurking behind the radiator! Leave them, my love, give them to me, unclench your teeth, good girl, give, GIVE! Oh, they're like magnets to dogs, aren't they?! Daily shower spray that only the conscientious use, Wash & Go, facial-mask sachets – caked mud, spooky self-heating and ones that peel off – a squelchy shower mat, a tired nail brush that's given up the will to live, lots of fancy hand wash in pump dispensers – bergamot and lime, aloe and silk, tangerine and coconut, fish and chips (there must have been a three-for-two offer from Boots recently) – talking scales that have been pushed into the corner so that their presence isn't too obvious or confrontational. On that note, when you're ready, it's . . .

☞ BIBLE TIME

Let's read 2 Kings 20.1–6.

> In those days Hezekiah became ill and was at the point of death. The prophet Isaiah son of Amoz went to him and said, 'This is what the LORD says: put your house in order, because you are going to die; you will not recover.'
>
> Hezekiah turned his face to the wall and prayed to the LORD, 'Remember, LORD, how I have walked before you faithfully and with wholehearted devotion and have done what is good in your eyes.' And Hezekiah wept bitterly.
>
> Before Isaiah had left the middle court, the word of the LORD came to him: 'Go back and tell Hezekiah, the ruler of my people, "This is what the LORD, the God of your father David, says: I have heard your prayer and seen your tears; I will heal you. On the third day from

now you will go up to the temple of the LORD. I will add fifteen years to your life. And I will deliver you and this city from the hand of the king of Assyria. I will defend this city for my sake and for the sake of my servant David."'

Read it through again.

So what's God saying?

Hezekiah had been a fine upstanding king in God's sight. He'd believed in God: not just believed he existed but believed in him as Creator, as Healer, as the giver of eternal life. God was King Hezekiah's life. He'd removed all the idols and altars that had been used to worship other gods and continued to live close to God during his reign. He tried to live a pure and clean life by walking in God's ways. Perhaps God's encouraging you to look at the cleanliness of *your* life?

If we look around at all that stuff in the bathroom, nearly everything we see is connected with cleanliness – we usually and mainly come into this room to get clean.

What does it mean to be clean in God's sight? Well, Hezekiah seemed to have done a pretty good job. He'd followed God's laws and done all the right things – but most other people weren't capable of that. So, long after Hezekiah's time, Jesus came. He took all our dirtiness on himself and took it with him when he died so that we could be clean in God's sight. So for us to be clean we need to believe in Jesus, to trust in what he's already done for us. Good news or what? It's a little like being told that you no longer have to shower or bath at all – ever – for the rest of your life! Brill! Think of the extra time you could stay in bed, the money to be saved on shower gel and bath mallows! Woohoo! You're clean!

But we do things wrong though, don't we – we still get dirty. Of course we do – we're human beings. Jesus understands that – that's why he came. So does that mean we can do what we like and get away with it? Yes: we have free will to do anything. However, if you believe in Jesus you naturally begin a relationship with him, to find out about him, what he's like, what advice he has for us. You can't be in a relationship with someone and not change. As a result Jesus shows us new ways of living and the things we do gradually fall in with his ways. When you do get something wrong, face it, don't ignore it; tell Jesus about it and ask him to help you change. Sometimes we may not *want* to change – ask Jesus to give you the will to want to change. In any case, once you've spoken with Jesus *you leave it with him*! Don't rake up past mistakes and dwell on how bad you must be. Remember: you're clean, you don't have to jump in the shower time and time again! Wash and go!

One more thing: if you don't want to be forever friends with fluoride or soulmates with a scrunchie, you avoid eating sweet things and stay away from coalmines, don't you? Is there any 'dirt' in your life that perhaps you need to distance yourself from? In my youth I wasn't a Christian and saw no harm in watching lots of horror movies and listening to tracks featuring sexually explicit lyrics. They did actually do me harm, instilling in me fear and a disrespect for others. So when I became a Christian the 'surface dirt' had to go – I studied theology and listened to Enya instead. Some of that dirt can go deep, so if it's there, body-wash it out and replace it with something clean, as King Hezekiah did.

ME: Right, Lil: come on, girl. Yes, just bring the underpants – I see the gusset's gone, so they're neither use nor ornament now. I'll meet you at church next, by the wheelie bins. Try not to be late – people might start offering me advice on history and architecture. Ta ra!

7

Go! When the going gets tough, the tough get going – to church?

☺ RELAX

My God, this is life and you are here. Wherever I may be, you're in my heart. Help me to know you, to love you. In Jesus' name. Amen.

☺ ABSORB

YOU: Entering a church is a bit like coming home for you, isn't it, Sister?

ME: Not at all. I feel great sadness walking into many churches. Their hard surfaces and straight lines make me feel uncomfortable.

It's a good job Lil's got her coat on, because this church is freezing! Silence. Sunlight beams through clear glass illuminating the dusty air. The stained glass produces dark corners. Hymn-book stacks, gnarled pews, fraying hassocks, tired leaflets, maroon and cream floor tiles. A gleaming brass lectern. Somebody's left their glasses case behind. Flaking wall plaster. Lil's devouring a spider. What's that smell – dust? Last week's hymn numbers are still up. A hot-water urn. Service books. Donations box. The organ's preciously enclosed and locked up. Dangerous steps up to the sanctuary. Lots of initials have been carved into the choir stalls. Thick prayer books with lots of coloured ribbons. Small, neat arrangements of chrysanthemums and carnations, whites and yellows. Can you see your breath as you exhale? We spot a white shape on the floor in the corner by the Gift Aid poster. It's Lil. She's found a mouse and is sitting there completely still and silent, waiting for it to appear. A wood pigeon warbles outside. At least here we don't have to worry if we've forgotten our Bible . . .

✍ BIBLE TIME

Let's read Acts 27.27–32.

> On the fourteenth night we were still being driven across the Adriatic Sea, when about midnight the sailors sensed they were approaching land. They took soundings and found that the water was forty metres deep. A short time later they took soundings again and found it was thirty metres deep. Fearing that we would be dashed against the rocks, they dropped four anchors from the stern and prayed for daylight. In an attempt to escape from the ship, the sailors let the lifeboat down into the sea, pretending they were going to lower some anchors from the bow. Then Paul said to the centurion and the soldiers, 'Unless these men stay with the ship, you cannot be saved.' So the soldiers cut the ropes that held the lifeboat and let it drift away.

Read it through again.

So what's God saying?

Those poor men yearned to jump ship. They'd spotted their escape route! However, someone speaks, tells them to stay right where they are. He's not even a member of the crew but they suddenly find themselves giving up trying to run away. They trust and persevere. Perhaps God wants to encourage *you* to stay the course?

I don't know about you but I've often found it difficult to persevere as a Christian and a member of the Church. I've thought about jumping ship. I haven't been a member long but I see arrogance, hypocrisy, hatred and pride within it. Then God reminds me of my own shortcomings, together with the holiness, goodness, love and peace that are also within the Church. *I* am the Church, as you are. So I persevere.

One of the most difficult times to persevere is if you see the need for change but others don't. Have you ever tried to initiate change in a parish church? It might simply be a new way of cleaning the brass or placing the flowers on a different window ledge, but it can awaken previously dormant aggression. The building itself with so many features set in place – pews, font, chests, table, altar, columns – sets the tone for an institution that can be very slow to move. It's difficult to persevere in an environment that can seem so stifling. However, God may have called you there, to work with those people you find frustrating, to bring about his will in that place. Perhaps you have to work with him to find a way? Perhaps you're wrong and are actually following your own desires rather than his? Plus, he will also have called you to grow. It may be that those you'd dearly love to throttle can teach you a few things, like the value of gentleness, patience and a reliance on God you would never feel the need for otherwise. Frank, Master of the Tea Urn, may take two hours to dismantle, clean and stow away the precious object every Sunday but, in this, God may be saying to you, 'Slow down, you don't need to stay on the motorway. I want you on a B road. You'll be able to hear me better.' Persevere and you might find yourself the agent of change, or you'll see the reason for the way things are.

Some of the stained-glass windows have, sadly, been smashed. The Church is often attacked and criticized from the 'outside' – in the general press, on television, by friends and relatives. Often the criticism is fair and understandable; at other times not. The way the Church operates and the way of life we believe Jesus teaches can be labelled old-fashioned or irrelevant. It can be very tempting for some of us to jump ship for an easier life, but God's called us to be his Church, to be his representatives on earth. As we wrestle with issues we must share them with him – he'll help us to persevere. We must also share them with other Christians if we can – I know how much 'lighter' I've felt after a rant and a latte with friends. Fellow travellers are invaluable. If we're questioning a particular issue it may also help to get back to what Jesus said in the Bible, to review his life and his teachings. Read the Letters in the New Testament too as they address topics the early Church wrestled with. Persevere.

Persevering in a particular vocation can be hard. You were certain you were called to do something and it was great at first. Now it's not so easy; the honeymoon period's over; the enthusiasm's fast disappearing. As a nun there are some days when I think, 'What on earth am I doing? How did I get here? Is there any value in living like this?' The first thing I do is remember the good times. I think back to when God called me and how I was certain it was the right path. Things had gone well for some time – until now. God could be testing me, testing my faith in order to strengthen it. Am I still willing to be faithful to him as the novelty of newness disappears? Do I think I would have lasted so long if it hadn't been right? I might think about moving on but it just doesn't seem right. Do I still feel a deep peace within even though I feel despondent? I carry on knowing that if he wants me to do something else he'll present me with the opportunity. Persevere.

One last thing: if you haven't got one already, I urge you to get a spiritual director or a 'soul friend'. When you're finding it difficult to stay the course, such people can be worth their weight in gold. They listen to any issues you might be having in your spiritual life and, with an ear to God, offer encouragement. Don't jump the ship you happily boarded, unless God's giving you a gangplank.

ME: Right: I'm going outside to warm up. Take a pew – mind the bat droppings. Lil and I will see you next in front of the telly for an episode of *Top Gear*. I think Lil's got a thing about Jeremy Clarkson's ankles, in that she'd like to taste them. Right now I think she's tasting a mouse – there's a tail hanging out of her mouth – and it's moving. Bye!!

8

Go! Revving up your passion in Top Gear!

☺ RELAX

Jesus, this is life and you are here. Bless this time with your presence. Nourish me with your living word. Amen.

☺ ABSORB

We're in front of the telly when all of a sudden *Top Gear* starts *vroom-vroom-vroom*! Cars, cars, cars! Zoom in camera! Pan to left! Screech those wheels! Burn that rubber! Chrome! Metallic! The need for speed! Kickin' up leaves on the lane! Twist! Turn! Spotlights! Camera focus in! Blur out! Smoke! Tyres! Jeans! Black jackets! White shirts! V8! Twin turbo! What's the torque, Stig? Off roadin'! What a hot hatch! Gosh, I'm out of breath already, and this is just the intro. High revs! Spoilers! Headlamps! Skids! Bhp! Mph! GTi! Couplings! Slingshot! Super smooth! Throttle! Back end! Shift time! Chassis! Calipers! Shut lines! DAB! Satnav! Park Assist! Safety Systems! Performance Packs! Put your pedal to the metal!

YOU: *(wafting me with a* Radio Times*)* Sister, you're overheating!

ME: It's OK, hombre, this habit has air-con!

Into the studio where it's dark, rather like a disused warehouse, with spotlights everywhere. Chequered flags, huge illuminated speedometers adorn the walls – this is a bit like walking into a younger brother's bedroom, only there aren't any Spitfires dangling from the ceiling. Three men in a uniform of black jacket, white shirt and jeans lounge on leather car seats drinking from plastic cups as if they're waiting for MOTs to finish. The glass-topped table seems to be propped up by an engine. In the gloom surrounding this ensemble is a crowd of men wearing mostly cargo pants and rugby shirts – there are token women if you look carefully. Lots of hand gestures by Mr Clarkson, who's unaware he's being watched by a trembling Jack Russell meditating on his ankles. When you're ready, it's . . .

✑ BIBLE TIME

Let's read Matthew 26.31–35.

> Then Jesus told them, 'This very night you will all fall away on account of me, for it is written: "I will strike the shepherd, and the sheep of the flock will be scattered." But after I have risen, I will go ahead of you into Galilee.' Peter replied, 'Even if all fall away on account of you, I never will.' 'Truly I tell you,' Jesus answered, 'this very night, before the cock crows, you will disown me three times.' But Peter declared, 'Even if I have to die with you, I will never disown you.' And all the other disciples said the same.

Read it through again.

So what's God saying?

Passionate, manly, full of bravado – that's Peter. And Jeremy Clarkson. 'Even if all fall away on account of you, I never will', declared Peter; 'Even if I have to die with you, I will never disown you.' This is raw passion. Does God wish to talk with you about your passion?

Like Peter, Jeremy and friends are passionate – passionate about cars. They don't just discuss boot space and paintwork, they get right into the nitty gritty – 'these seats massage you as you drive!', 'this car is about as interesting as an insurance man's trousers', 'the ABS here is spot on'. This is non-stop chat about cars; this is raw passion! I've been in some churches where any mention of Jesus in post-service conversation causes anxious looks and a change of subject (usually to the quality of the Jammie Dodgers or the skull and crossbones on the vicar's popsocks). Passion? We can learn much from Jeremy.

So God might be asking you to think about your passions. What are you passionate about? Is there something you love doing? A friend of mine is passionate about films. He subscribes to *Film Review* and has an informal rating for each director. My mum is crazy about animals, especially dogs. If she hears of a stray she'll do all she can to find it a home or else she'll take it home herself. Passion. Passions are important because they're a big part of who you are. They're life-giving. They help make life 'life'. We each have different passions. One of my passions has four legs and a beard and is sitting in front of the telly drooling over Jeremy. Lil is so much fun and gives me great joy. God may have given you a passion, so make room for it. Don't crowd it out with work. It may be that he'd like to work through it in some kind of ministry. Teaching, perhaps, or art, making greetings cards, knitting, scuba diving, ironing (ironing?!) – what's your pash?

Perhaps you're passionate about collecting things? Another friend of mine was mad about books. She only had a small bungalow but her back room was full of books. Many people love little ornaments and knick-knacks, buying them in bulk from car boot sales. Beware! If you're a collector, God might just want to know if you love your collectables more than him. My book-loving friend had been over this with God. If her beloved collectables were destroyed, or she had to give them up because she was called to be a missionary in India, she knew she could – and would – part company with them. She loved God more than her books. So watch out: he's a jealous God and wants to take pole position on the starting grid of your life!

Perhaps you're passionate about a person, a friend or a celebrity? It's all too easy to turn someone like Becks, for instance, into a god. He's got money, power, influence, status, good looks, great footy skills – but God says, 'Hey, I made him. How much greater am I? Look at ME! *I* want to be your number 1!' Is there someone you see as a role model? Someone you see as perfect? Creations cannot live up to our high expectations; it's unfair to put them on a pedestal. You're setting them up for a fall and yourself too. Once again God is shouting, 'Look at ME!'

Are you passionate about yourself? Do you think you're the best thing since sliced bread? Are you working full-out to climb that corporate ladder? Do you really, really, really want to make it on to the Rich List? God might want a word with you about such passions. He might ask you to redirect them to work for him and for others instead of yourself. Up for it?

Lastly, are you passionate about God? He wants you to be. If you're not and want to be, ask him to help you. I did a few months ago. I yelled at a crucifix, 'I want to be passionate for you!' A few months later I was telling Reverend Mother how I'd discovered my passion – nothing to do with God answering my prayer, of course. If you're passionately in love you usually know the other person quite well – 'Aah, I just love the way he picks his toenails and inadvertently lets me see the contents of his mouth while eating.' Passion is heart stuff, so to be passionate about God you need to know him well. Jesus shows us what God's like in the Gospels. Read them slowly; spend quality time with God on your own; tell God about how you feel and about what's happening in your life; leave room for him to speak; just be; ask him to fill you with his Holy Spirit. Clutch down, first gear, rev up to be as passionate as Peter and Jeremy! Go, baby, go!!

And hey, by the way: God's passionate about YOU. Diggit?

ME: Lil! LIL!!! Come on, saliva chops. The library's our next stop. You'll find me in the coffee shop opposite the Talking Books section. (Have you ever heard one talk? I haven't.) Until then, farewell, dear friend!

9

Go! Longing for God in the library

☺ RELAX

Lord God, this is life and you are here. Take from me my worries and fears and fill me with your Holy Spirit as I read your sacred word. In Jesus' name. Amen.

☺ ABSORB

Aah, the quietness and calmness of the library. Lil's enjoying her own peace as she's in retreat today – '2 Timothy for Terriers' – with nine others. Begins at 10.30 a.m. with water and biscuits; silence throughout the day; ending with water, Jumbones and tennis balls at 3.30 p.m. Back to the library. Books – the efforts of so many, their tears, their experiences, their lives, so many hopes, all condensed within two covers and a contents page. A baby cries, others gurgle in the crèche. We plonk down into comfy sofas – this is a modern library. Dark greys merge with neon green, orange and red – this *is* a modern library. Hushed conversations. The rustle of a broadsheet being read. There's an IT learning zone. The café! You can return your books without interacting with a human. Sssshhhh! Lots of flat-screen monitors. Occasional young people in chinos with square glasses, jumpers, stubble and 'just got out of bed' hair – and that's just the girls. Trendy

IKEA swivel chairs with metallic mesh backs. The buggy park's empty – that's why it's so quiet. The 'skhsssssshhhhh!' marks the birth of a cappuccino. An elderly gent is surfing the net – superb. Smartphones. Headphones. Local notices. A restrained but cheery conversation about fridge magnets and what you can now put in your recycling bin. Novels. The silence is too much for one toddler as she begins a temper tantrum. 'Deep breaths', breathes Mum, 'calm down. What's the problem? Well, these are your options . . .' Poor child – she's an adult already. Funny yet profound messages in fun fonts adorn the walls. The clinking of distant spoons and cups and the faint whiff of a latte.

YOU: *(whisper)* Do you fancy a coffee, Sister?

ME: *(whisper)* Does the Pope pray? Of course I do. But we have to look intelligent first – get your Bible out.

✒ BIBLE TIME

Let's read Isaiah 58.1–3 (now remember that these Bible readings were chosen at random).

> Shout it aloud, do not hold back. Raise your voice like a trumpet. Declare to my people their rebellion and to the descendants of Jacob their sins. For day after day they seek me out; they seem eager to know my ways, as if they were a nation that does what is right and has not forsaken the commands of its God. They ask me for just decisions and seem eager for God to come near them. 'Why have we fasted,' they say, 'and you have not seen it? Why have we humbled ourselves, and you have

not noticed?' Yet on the day of your fasting, you do as you please and exploit all your workers.

Read it through again.

So what's God saying?

I tried so hard not to burst out laughing when I read that Bible passage. In the silence of a library God tells us to shout aloud! Raise your voice like a trumpet! Don't hold back! One thing that God is getting across here is his sense of humour.

God is saying, through Isaiah, that the people seemingly long for him, they seek him out saying they're eager to know his ways, but actually, in the end, they do what they like. It's no wonder they can't find him. Are they *really* looking, *really* longing for him? It's as if they give God a token nod every now and then but look to satisfy their desires elsewhere. We don't do that, do we? Do we?

So what might God be saying to you here? Well, look at all these books – there's fiction, non-fiction, religion, philosophy, art, photography, children's, reference, self-improvement, travel, crime, computing, languages and more. You could be forgiven for thinking that all the answers to your longings are somewhere in here. They're not. Some may be, but give God a chance to say something too. Your choice of book may reveal an inner longing that you should also be talking to God about. Let me give you some examples.

We love adventure! I'd love to be Sister Indiana Jones who in her latest epic escapes from Father Evil by abseiling down the Shard, careering through gunshots on a stolen Vespa, surfboarding the 5.01 p.m. from Victoria to Portsmouth and Southsea, leaping on to a disability scooter while dodging self-detonating flying pizzas, arriving home just in time for Evening Prayer. Whew! Fiction, comics and novels are marvellous; they take us out of our lives for a while if things get a bit bland or heavy. However, don't ignore Jesus if you want adventure. Just read the life of any saint to find out what can happen! Have you heard about missionary Gladys Aylward? Born in 1902, Gladys worked as a housemaid who dreamed of missionary work in China. When she was 30 she spent all her savings getting there. She took in orphans and, although wounded during a Japanese invasion, safely led over a hundred of them across mountainous terrain. She said 'yes' to God and embarked on the adventure of a lifetime. So if you have an adventurous streak, take it to God and wait for him to lead you.

The self-improvement section – *Master Microsoft Word in a Weekend*. This is possible if you don't do anything else during those two days, like de-fluff your sofa, dead-head your roses, bath the dog, stock up on Ben & Jerry's at Asda and attend a car boot sale. Oh, and go to church of course. On Monday morning you can stride into your cubicle looking fonts and footers firmly in the face. That's genuinely good. However, don't ignore God for advice on self-improvement. Read 1 John. I did recently. I've shelved my copy of *Get to Grips with Gujarati* for now. I'm asking Jesus to help me love others more.

Biographies. Now there are some lovely accounts of the lives of noted celebs like Elizabeth Taylor, Arnold Schwarzenegger, Dawn French and Bob the street cat. Perhaps we're looking for inspiration? It could be there are problems in our own lives that we don't want to face. We'd rather read about other people and fantasize about how perfect their lives must be. If that's the case, once again, don't forget that God needs to be consulted here too. Let Jesus inspire you by reading about his miracles – after all, Rod Stewart can't walk on water. If you've got probs then acknowledge them and trot them all out to God, who's waiting to hear you. Your life story's important.

Aah, romance! Get your nose into a Mills & Boon and float away on flushing cheeks, pouting lips and heaving bosoms. Are you yearning for love yourself? Do you long to kick up leaves with someone in the park while your heart beats with passion? Once again, don't ignore God here! God loves you and he might be asking you to think about that, to accept it into your heart. A friend came round yesterday in tears because she felt she'd let God down and that he wouldn't love her any more. We are so used to conditional love – if I do that they'll love me. There's nothing you can do to make God love you more. No: God's love isn't the same as human love, and constantly delving into romantic novels could close your ears to him shouting, 'Hey! Don't forget me, *I* love you!'

Don't get paranoid – enjoy your books, but don't do what the Israelites did: ignore God in your everyday, immerse yourself in books and then have a good moan about him! Sermon over.

ME: *(whispering)* OK, I'm going to leave you here to chat with God while I enjoy a latte. We're meeting in the kitchen next. Yay! Lil and I love cooking. Did you hear about the crying biscuit? He was upset because his dad had been a wafer so long. And the rhubarb taken into custardy? Adios, amigo!

10

Go! Praising God at the breakfast bar!

———•◆•———

☺ RELAX

Lord God, this is life and you are here. I praise you for being my God. Still my soul, open my eyes, ears and heart to receive you. In Jesus' name. Amen.

☺ ABSORB

The kitchen! The heart of the home, why is it the unofficial meeting place in a house? Lil associates the kitchen with Bonios, her fave treat. She's now decided to perform her 'dinosaur act' where she rears up on her hind legs like a Tyrannosaurus Rex and pounds the lino with her front feet – this means she wants a Bonio.

YOU: Shall I give her a bicky?
ME: Mmm . . . yes. Take one for yourself while you're at it; it looks as though we've run out of digestives.

Fridge magnets that warn you of the quality of the cooking that goes on here, a mismatch of mugs, the microwave, a colander, serving spoons, spatulas and a cheese grater. A novelty biscuit barrel, bulging bread bin, a crumb-covered toaster. Suddenly an owl hoots from somewhere – must mean it's noon (a novelty birdsong-effect clock). The well-used self-cleaning oven which, by the look of it, has downed its Mr Muscle and gone on strike. A fridge freezer hums. A chicken-shaped timer awaits its next job – there are lots of novelty items in here. A kitchen roll stands to attention on its stick. A chrome tree prolongs the death of a sole banana. A sock has clearly leapt for its life from the washing machine – it's a wonder Lil hasn't had that yet. Lots of surfaces, scored with naughty knife marks – no wonder the bread board's immaculate. Neatly aligned cupboards hide their mysterious contents. A chrome pedal bin. Oven gloves never used, tea towels over-used. The fresh scent of 'Sunshine Days' fabric conditioner. A rarely empty, well-loved kettle. A Jack Russell with its nose in a sock. Are we ready to read?

✑ BIBLE TIME

Let's read Psalm 147.1–7.

> Praise the LORD.
> How good it is to sing praises to our God, how
>   pleasant and fitting to praise him!
> The LORD builds up Jerusalem; he gathers the
>   exiles of Israel.
> He heals the broken-hearted and binds up their
>   wounds.
> He determines the number of the stars and calls
>   them each by name.
> Great is our Lord and mighty in power; his
>   understanding has no limit.

The LORD sustains the humble but casts the
    wicked to the ground.
Sing to the LORD with grateful praise; make
    music to our God on the harp.
He covers the sky with clouds; he supplies the earth
    with rain and makes grass grow on the hills.
He provides food for the cattle and for the young
    ravens when they call.
His pleasure is not in the strength of the horse,
    nor his delight in the legs of the warrior;
the LORD delights in those who fear him, who
    put their hope in his unfailing love.

Read it through again.

So what's God saying?

This is a beautiful psalm of praise, a 'Laudate' (praise) psalm
that we often pray during Matins, our morning prayer time.
It's chock-full of praises to God – for healing, the gathering
together of exiles, for his power and for his unfailing love.
If that's not enough, for the creation of the stars, the skies,
the earth, rain, grass, food – phew, I'm all praised out! Now
I'm no Hercule Poirot, but is God trying to draw your
attention to 'praise' by any chance?

The kitchen has to be one of my fave rooms – is it one of
yours? If there was ever a room to praise God in, this is it!
Why? Because there are so many elements at work here. It
shouts out lovely things to me, like 'nourishment, warmth,
coffee, new beginnings, life, love, Bonios'! But before I begin
levitating on to the cooker hood, let's take a peek at praise.

Until I became a Christian I associated praise with patting
a schoolboy on his head and telling him how good his crayon

drawings of the Houses of Parliament were; or saying, 'Well done' to Lil when she was sick on the newspaper rather than the carpet. One often hears 'Praise the Lord' in some churches for seemingly no apparent reason, as though it's an automatic add-on to the end of a sentence, like 'D'ya know what I mean?' So I used to find praise a bit of a mystery and certainly didn't praise God for anything. If I was going to praise I wanted to mean it; and anyway, does God need us to give him a grateful wink every now and then; does he need to hear us say, 'Well done for creating Bird's – no, not the winged types, the custard'? And you can't really praise anyone for anything until you know something about them and what they've done, can you? Well, as my relationship with God deepened, two things happened. First, I realized that praise is an essential part of any relationship, that it's an appreciation of another 'being'. Second, as I recognized God as the Creator of all, I found I wanted to praise him for loads of things! Praise came to mean more of a heartfelt 'Thank you' or a 'Wow – look what you've done!' than a pat on the back. And in a kitchen one can go praise crazy!

The kitchen, to me, is a 'morning' room – we hop, skip, jump or slump into this room first thing to get nourishment, whether a full English or one, or two – or three – bowls of Crunchy Nut Cornflakes, maybe even granary toast with Nutella. Coupled with a latte or an OJ, these things smell and taste soooo good and they recharge your batteries for a new day! So for tasty food and nourishment, praise God!

Lil loves mornings because once she's up she waters the garden and goes back to bed – she enjoys her creature comforts after her early days in a rescue centre. For me, mornings mean new beginnings, daytime, light, awakening, a bringing to life, fresh hopes – if there's a problem, it could be solved by tea-time! To many, the darkness of night can make any issues seem ten times worse. So every morning, put your arms up in the air and praise God for a new day – go on, I will if you will!

What about cooking? Now, I have exploded eggs in microwaves and lost sausages in an oven – a trayful was put in and on removal all had disappeared (they had rolled off into the back of the oven and were found a few days later resembling cremated faggots). Preparing a meal or baking a cake is an act of love, and it's amazing – mix marge, sugar, flour and eggs together, give it some heat and, hey presto, something edible! And we can't forget that symbol of comfort and love – the kettle. 'Come and have a cuppa.' 'Do you take sugar? Any milk?' For love, comfort and creativity, praise God!

The kettle, the microwave, the washing machine, the fridge freezer, Auntie Morag's gift of 20 'Poachets' for non-messy egg poaching – they're all objects that go to make the kitchen a 'helpful' room: you don't have to do everything yourself. So for the gift of clever people designing modern technology, praise God!

Praising God and seeing him in the everyday is good, but don't forget to praise him for being 'him' (or 'her'), the Creator who made you and loves you.

ME: I don't mean to be rude, but I think your nose has got longer, and I can see you're starting to pant. How many dog biscuits did you have? Come on, Lil – we'll see you next on the touchline at the football match in the park. United are playing – apparently they 'Winalot'. Oops – sorry. Bye.

11

Go! Eternal life: it's a game of two halves!

———•:•:•———

☺ RELAX

Lord God, this is life and you are here, even in the hustle and bustle of sport. Above the cheers, quieten my heart that I may hear your voice. In Jesus' name. Amen.

☉ ABSORB

We've reluctantly trodden half a mile through a sodden recreation ground to a local football match, dutifully pulled along and encouraged by Lil, who I think is quite keen to meet up with a particularly attractive poodle (she likes bouffant hair). It's damp and cold and I don't know about you, but I would rather be in a warm Costa coffee shop. The pitch isn't nice and green like you see on *Match of the Day*; it's more mud than grass, and full of stud marks. The refreshing scent of wet grass is tempered by the aggressive fumes of Deep Heat. There are no nets in either goal. The players are wearing different-coloured tabards, not kits. If you're a spectator you're vulnerable – watch your head! Play starts with a dodgy whistle. Flurries of wildly inaccurate shots – there's more slicing going on here than in a butcher's. Man on!

Half an hour later: there's an attack; I think a goal's been scored although there's no kissing or cuddling, just manly slaps and approving grunts. 'Lil, come here!' Oh dear, she's lunged as the ball's come near. Dog on! A great dribbler, she might improve the team. Ooh, there's a tussle going on along the touchline – shoves, kicks, a shirt's pulled. Ref! The air's turned blue with the language. Mmm – nice waft of coffee coming from the sub's bench. Neon-coloured boots bearing huge Nike swooshes are worn in a vain effort to enhance performance. Someone's leaping like a salmon – was that a goal? It was! I'm missing the slow-mos and the action replays we see on telly. It's half-time, thank goodness. There were a couple of good goals there, nice. Sorry: what's the score? 5–4? Oh, I must have missed, er, some of those . . .

YOU: I heard that you play footy, Sister.
ME: I try to. My keepy-uppy record is 24 – Lil's is 302. She's recently been approached by the Blues.
YOU: What, Chelsea?!!
ME: No, Barking FC.

When you're ready, it's . . .

🖝 BIBLE TIME

Let's read Isaiah 14.9–15.

The realm of the dead below is all astir to meet you at your coming; it rouses the spirits of the departed to greet you – all those who were leaders in the world; it makes them rise from their thrones – all those who were kings over the nations. They will all respond, they will say to you, 'You also have become weak, as we are; you have become like us.' All your pomp has been brought down to the grave, along with the noise of your harps; maggots are spread out beneath you and worms cover you. How you have fallen from heaven, morning star, son of the dawn! You have been cast down to the earth, you who once laid low the nations! You said in your heart, 'I will ascend to the heavens; I will raise my throne above the stars of God; I will sit enthroned on the mount of assembly, on the utmost heights of Mount Zaphon. I will ascend above the tops of the clouds; I will make myself like the Most High.' But you are brought down to the realm of the dead, to the depths of the pit.

Read it through again.

So what's God saying?

It's important to be aware that this shocking passage is part of a taunt that Isaiah prophesies Israel will say against the oppressive king of Babylon. The overriding theme is death. Death is a natural part of life but, as Christians, we aren't 'maggot and worm' people, we're eternal-life people. Perhaps God's saying something like, 'Death is not the full-time but the *half*-time whistle.' We're born at kick-off and the first half here on earth is full of action – as we'll see. At half-time we come off the field of life – we die, we pass away – to continue living and playing the second half but in a different way. Eternal life: it's a game of two halves – fancy a kick-about?

56

OK, so Nike Tiempo boots in Sunburst Red don't exactly go with an Air Force Blue habit – style's never been my thing. Lil's looking good in her Adidas Predators. 'On the 'ead, son!' Lil flicks the ball up with her nose; I bring it under control and curl it beautifully – into someone's lunchbox. 'Sorry, mate!' Life's full of little failures, but are they failures? If I hadn't successfully hit those sarnies with my shot I wouldn't know how to alter my next attempt at goal. Learn from your little slip-ups and thank God for them!

So it's me and Lil against you. You come in for a tackle, grab my veil – hey, Ref, did you see that?! Life's littered with tussles and opposition. Just do your best and let God do the rest – keep on lifting up your troubles to God; don't stop!

Ref's blown for a free kick. I'm placing the ball carefully – Lil, leave it! A few steps back, concentrate . . . When opportunities seem to come your way take them to God and listen to what he has to say. What gives you peace in your heart? What's life-giving to you?

I take the free kick, bend it like Beckham and it floats gracefully through the goal – YES, it's a winner!!! Lil and I boogie in the box – woohoo! Cha, cha, cha! Cha, cha, cha! Yee-hah! There are times of consolation in life when excitement and joy abound! Woo! Ride high on these moments and praise God! Remember them because you'll need them for strength in the future.

We play on and I slide in for a tackle, taking your legs from under you. 'Sorry!' I feel really bad about that. You're awarded a penalty. We all make mistakes; we're only human. Acknowledge them, tell God about them and ask him to help you not to make them again. Ask his forgiveness, receive it and move on. Don't wallow in self-pity or despair: you've been forgiven, you've asked for help, now play on!

You cannonball a power-shot into the net to score – it's a draw! You tango on the touchline. Lil and I sheepishly applaud your skill. It's not easy to rejoice with others; it depends on whether we like the person or not, doesn't it? Someone else's success can stir up feelings of jealousy and resentment that perhaps we didn't know we had. If this is so, it's often a case of setting your will to be pleased for the person. Once done, that may lift us up and out of our negative feelings; if not, we must take it to God in prayer and allow him to help us explore why we feel this way.

The half-time whistle blows! Well done all! We wearily trudge off the field of life to the bench. Remember: we've finished our earthly efforts – we've 'died' – and can now rest up for a bit. Aah, heavenly Jaffas for us and a Bacon Sizzler chewie for Lil. Lucozade Sport – just the thing; it's a time of reparation and renewal.

The second half? Well, we come back on to the pitch with new bodies; we're not quite the same as we were. What the game will be like I don't know – if you're expecting me to go into details of what life in heaven will be like, you're going to be disappointed. I only know it'll be brill and that God will be there as team captain. Padre Pio declared that his real mission would begin after he had died. He was right – hordes of miracles were attributed to his intercession after his death in 1968; he was subsequently made a saint in 2002. So we play on into eternity! Cowabunga!

ME: Phew, we're bushwhacked. I don't know about you, but Lil and I didn't warm up, so we're going to be walking like robots tomorrow. Next session is in front of the telly with *Antiques Roadshow*. Talking of antiques, I feel like an ancient relic at the moment – Deep Heat's on offer at Boots. Bye!

12

Go! God brings his gifts to Antiques Roadshow

———◦•◦———

☺ RELAX

Lord God, this is life and you are here. Warm my heart with your love, open my soul to receive you. In Jesus' name. Amen.

☉ ABSORB

Yeah! It's a Sunday evening and *Roadshow*'s on! Woo! Even Lil's excited – ah, it's because she's smelled the tuna and cucumber sandwiches, that's why. That familiar and elegant intro music calls us to attention and we settle down by watching folk in quaint English villages place their antiques in Morris Minor convertibles, smiling with satisfaction at their purchases – what a wonderful world.

YOU: Aah, this is perfect, isn't it, Sister? A summer
        Sunday evening, the *Roadshow* on, yummy sarnies
        and a pot of Yorkshire Tea. Perfect.

ME: Er, I'm afraid it isn't. Lil's just thrown up into your
        moccasins. Carry on watching while I get a cloth.
        I thought I saw her chomping grass earlier – or
        perhaps a tuna and cucumber sandwich.

The lovely Fiona Bruce is introducing the show. Why do I suddenly feel intelligent, taking an interest in the history of a flaky wall? Blue skies, sunshine, green lawns, men in Pringle jumpers, hoodies, farmers, jeans, ladies in Laura Ashley, murmuring queues, everyone has a bag. The experts are in conservative dress with manicures for quality close-up shots (otherwise they get complaints from beauty groups), hallmarks, maker's marks, 'I bought it in a car boot for 10p, ya' know', porcelain, portraits, automatons, 'Do you have it insured?', jewellery, furniture, 'What can you tell me about it?', Wedgwood, Rococo, Lalique, 'It's of sentimental value, I'm not interested in how much it's worth' (of course you're not), Beswick, Fabergé, Apple. Apple?! Oh, it's my friend's twenty-first-century tablet; she'll be thrilled when I tell her how much it's worth.

Sorry, I'm getting carried away – when we're ready, it's . . .

✐ BIBLE TIME

Let's read Psalm 19.1–5.

> The heavens declare the glory of God;
>> the skies proclaim the work of his hands.
> Day after day they pour forth speech;
>> night after night they reveal knowledge.
> They have no speech, they use no words;
>> no sound is heard from them.
> Yet their voice goes out into all the earth,
>> their words to the ends of the world.
> In the heavens God has pitched a tent for the sun.
> It is like a bridegroom coming out of his chamber,
>> like a champion rejoicing to run his course.

Read it through again.

So what's God saying?

This is a beautiful psalm, the first line of which could be changed to read '*Antiques Roadshow* declares the glory of God; those blue skies proclaim the work of his hands.' The *Roadshow* is an absolute smorgasbord of people and things that, if we consider them, declare God's glory. Yes, there's the danger of worshipping material things and flogging your Ming vase to buy a Range Rover Evoque, but there's also a lot of God here. I feel that's what he's saying. So let's join the queue and find out where the *real* treasure lies.

Who else could tell you the ins and outs of an artist's life but a *Roadshow* expert? 'Of course, he painted this during the "Quiche" period of his life, when he couldn't even pick up a brush before eating some and, as you can see, the palette of this piece is reminiscent of salmon and broccoli.' Their knowledge is amazing. The owner of the piece cannot but sit there transfixed as the life history of her ugly bronze, complete with dents because it's been used as a doorstop, is revealed. Who would have guessed it had sat on some Marquis's mantelpiece? The patience of the experts too – how many times must they have heard, 'I can't really tell you anything much, only that it came down from my great-great-grandmother'? Their knowledge and manner are gifts we can praise the Giver of all good things for.

And there's that family feel to the *Roadshow*, isn't there? Mum spreads the Dinky-toy collection out on the table while the children stand stiffly behind not saying anything in case that fire engine they bit the wheels off happens to be worth £3,000. Sometimes children bring in their own treasures – like a rare cast-off Action Man *without* moving eyes – and profess more knowledge than the expert. We see so many objects that have been passed down through generations, don't we? There are family paintings, Granddad's war memorabilia, Auntie's flying ducks – they're all there. Some of us may not have happy family feelings, but that model of what it means to be family can be seen, and that's something to thank God for.

Sculptors, carpenters, jewellers, potters, painters – each cherished object brought trembling in front of the camera is the work of a gifted person. It doesn't matter whether it's a Clarice Cliff or a Connie Cockersthwaite – somebody, somewhere has put heart and soul into making something of value, whether sentimental or monetary. Perhaps God's given you artistic gifts – are you using them? In the busy-ness of our world, hobbies and 'arty' pursuits can easily be shoved out – they're important, they're gifts given to you, so don't abuse them, *use* them!

How many times on the *Roadshow* do we hear, 'Well, my mother gave it to me when she died'? A lot of the antiques we see have been given to their owners. Gifts are a great way of saying, 'I love you' or 'I value you'. Of course we all want to see the object that's worth £100,000, but sentimental value is – how can we put it – priceless? Gifts given in love are gifts of God.

How about gifts received? Don't you feel good when someone gives you something? You can wake up feeling like a sloth with a hangover, receive a gift and consequently turn into a lamp-swinging lemur – you feel valued, don't you, you feel loved? I love it when a twinkly-eyed expert proclaims, 'In my 39 years in the furniture business I have never seen dovetails like those. You've made my day!' The expert's spirits are roused and there's real joy in his or her heart! Such feelings are to be treasured and God should be thanked for a life as brilliant as this!

Now it's very right and true that we shouldn't worship created things, only the Creator. However, created things can be *windows* to God, helping to lift our souls to him. Marvel at the reds of cranberry glass, the subtle flesh-tones in a watercolour, the brilliance of a Royal Doulton, the simple charm of a Beswick. You can almost feel the atmosphere of a *Roadshow*. It's nice and pleasant, isn't it? One can enjoy tea with the vicar of the parish afterwards perhaps. Those shows not held in the local sports centre bask in sunshine under brilliant blue skies. There's the gentle undercurrent of laughter and conversation coming from the queues. Have you ever appreciated the roughness of a Troika or cuddled a Steiff? All these things enliven our God-given senses; the secret is to look *past* them, to the One who gave the gifts to the jeweller or the cabinet maker, and to thank him for how they enrich your life!

ME: Right, we're off. Well, I think Lil actually is *off*; I'm really sorry about your slippers. Catch you next at the park – at least it's more 'vomit-friendly' there. TTFN! Are you sure that's not a Meissen, by the way?

13

Go! Kissing in the park – with God

------◆◆◆------

☺ RELAX

Creator God, this is life and you are here. Thank you for all
you have made. Help me to grow in response to your love.
In Jesus' name. Amen.

☺ ABSORB

Aah, the park, the space! The freshness of the air! We stand,
legs akimbo, arms aloft and breathe in until we can breathe
in no more . . . and then exhale . . . aah. Tease out any tension,
and chill. Lil looks bemused. Listen to that silence. Of course
it isn't *really* silence, but there are no cars, no lawnmowers,
just sweet birdsong, our feathered friends praising God.
A slight breeze, cooling the warmth, rustles the oak-tree
leaves high above. As we walk, slowly, the earthy smell of
damp foliage flies up our nostrils. Look at the thousands
of shades of green and brown. A gravel path lies ahead of
us dictating our way. Lil's in paradise, nose in the heather,
squatting every now and again to leave her calling card. Cycle
tracks can be seen if you look hard enough, along with the
occasional dog poo. In the distance we espy what looks like
a Schnauzer taking his owner for a walk. Suddenly the lead
goes taut and Lil's stopped, trying to position her hind feet

in order to create a firm base for a delicate manoeuvre – a bit like golfers do when they're preparing to putt.

ME: I think you have Lil's bags. Please could you pass me one?
YOU: *(sniff, sniff)* They're not perfumed, are they?
ME: Yes, 'Moroccan Mystery', I think. Five hundred for £2. Just make 100 per cent sure there are no holes.

When we're ready, it's . . .

☞ BIBLE TIME

Let's read Galatians 2.11–14.

> When Cephas came to Antioch, I opposed him to his face, because he stood condemned. For before certain men came from James, he used to eat with the Gentiles. But when they arrived, he began to draw back and separate himself from the Gentiles because he was afraid of those who belonged to the circumcision group. The other Jews joined him in his hypocrisy, so that by their hypocrisy even Barnabas was led astray. When I saw that they were not acting in line with the truth of the gospel, I said to Cephas in front of them all, 'You are a Jew, yet you live like a Gentile and not like a Jew. How is it, then, that you force Gentiles to follow Jewish customs?'

Read it through again.

So what's God saying?

I think God must be saying something like, 'Why do my children have to make things so complicated?!' It all started

so simply – Peter hanging out with the Gentiles. Great.
Then things got complicated. Why? Fear came in when a
gang of dudes sent by James turned up. Peter stopped
chilling with the Gentile crew; it didn't seem like such a
good idea after all. Being a main man, others took notice
and copied him. Enter Paul, who gave Peter an earful, reminding him that Gentile Christians didn't need to follow Jewish
Christian customs. So God might have said, 'Why did you
have to confuse the scene?' With our fears and feelings we
can change something simple into something chaotic. It's
human. It's a wrap.

Because we humans can make life so difficult for ourselves,
we need our open spaces. This park gives us a feeling of
freedom. There are no everyday noises, sights and smells,
and we can be on our own away from the complications
other humans can sometimes bring into our lives. There are
no messy relationships or mind games going on here; things
simply exist in their natural order as God intended. Simplicity
is an aspect of God. Our relationship with him has no need
to be complex, with an abundance of prayer formulas and
devotions. When God speaks with us it's simple and direct.
We feel it's him in our hearts. Complication and chaos can
block the air waves, so avoid them if you can. God's put the
beauty into park life – simplicity. Want some in *your* life?
OK, let's KISS – Keep It Simple Sweetheart.

Example: you don't see a foxglove telling a forget-me-not
how it was wee-ed on by a dog and proclaiming that 'The
beast must have been as big as a *house*!' do you? Exaggeration
is a complication, a little form of deceit. We exaggerate in
order to convince our friends we have a really interesting
story. In wanting to be accepted and popular we complicate

the issue. Remember Roy Walker's catchphrase, 'Say what you see'? So KISS.

Gorse doesn't gossip, does it? Gossip usually includes the sharing of something negative about someone. Talking about another person behind their back is extremely hurtful and malicious. It spreads lies, anxieties and, if we've half a conscience, guilt whenever we see the 'victim'. It harms relationships. It complicates life. Don't do it. Instead, KISS.

Lil's staring out a Red Admiral. Fluttering its wings on that lupin, it's not saying, 'If Terry the Turquoise Blue comes this way, tell him you haven't seen me', is it? Course not. Have you ever been asked to tell little white lies like this? I must have driven my family crazy when I became a Christian. I would sometimes hear, 'If the phone rings, can you answer it? And if it's so-and-so, tell her I'm not in.' My answer to that would be, 'No. Please don't ask me to lie.' Annoying? Yes, but a lie's a lie and white lies can be the beginnings of bigger ones. They complicate. So KISS.

Another seemingly harmless form of complication is false praise. I have to say that since I've been mixing in Christian circles I've witnessed many instances of this. Example: someone sings a hymn and makes several mistakes. Afterwards the singer is told he or she did really well – end of story. This leaves the singer and others confused.com. Now I'm not saying that person should be told, 'Man, you were pants', but people need to have their mistakes pointed out while at the same time being encouraged (very important). They'll grow, and others will know what *they* need to be aiming for. Some Christians are so afraid of not being nice that they don't want to confront anyone or anything in any way. Such fear of confrontation complicates. So KISS.

You only have to glance at a Problem Page to see how complicated we can make life. Most complications are caused by deceit – for example, having a fling while married. It's not always easy to be truthful, but it's God's way and that's not always plain sailing. Be honest with yourself and others – up front, above board. That's simplicity. That's park life. So KISS.

ME: OK, bambino, Lil and I are going to hotfoot it out of here to leave you to enjoy KISSing. For our next session we'll be collecting you in 'Cleopatra', our clapped-out navy-blue Renault. Don't forget your Bible and a bit of Dutch courage, because Lil's driving. Only kidding! It's a manual and her licence is only for automatics. Catch you later, gladiator!

14

Go! Think car! Think God!

☺ RELAX

Lord God, this is life and you are here. In the stillness of
these moments, open my heart that I may hear your voice.
In Jesus' name. Amen.

☺ ABSORB

I don't know about you but the first thing I notice when
I get into a car is the smell – the 'car' smell of plastic,
shampoo, leather and a Magic Tree air freshener dangling
from the rear-view mirror. Sweet wrappers in the door pocket.
A fly head-butting the windscreen as it tries to escape. Lil's
waiting for it to drop as she straddles the handbrake with
her face up against an open air vent. Her beard and eyebrows
flutter in the draught and I'm reminded of that famous scene
in *Titanic* when Kate Winslet stands at the front of the ship,
arms outstretched, hair flowing in the breeze. Gosh – what
a bizarre connection to make. A splodge of Blu-Tack on the
dash – one places one's AA route map on it to make a very
basic, but effective, satnav. A Tesco bag stuffed underneath the
glove box. There's lots of black; the seats are dark grey and
blue. A weary tax-disc holder. Dust, dirt, biscuit crumbs –
little collections where the vacuum cleaner attachment can't

get. Birdsong. A rain-speckled windscreen. Comfortable velour seats. Mirrors. Well-worn pedals. An 'airbag' sign – it resembles someone working out with a fitness ball. A 'No Smoking' sign next to a 'No Back-seat Driving' sign. Dog-eared – sorry Lil – warning stickers. J-cloths stuffed in a door pocket. A tin of boiled sweets. Lots of symbols – hazard lights, indicators, headlamps, seatbelts, horn, heated mirrors. Levers, handles, wheels, buttons everywhere.

YOU: Lil doesn't get carsick, does she?
ME: No, no. She loves Vauxhalls . . .
     (a hanging silence)
YOU: But this is a Renault . . . isn't it?
ME: Uh, yes. Yes, it is actually a Renault. Look, don't worry; she smiles before she does it. You'll know in good time. I think we'd better read, yes? It's . . .

BIBLE TIME

Let's read Hosea 7.1–7.

> Whenever I would heal Israel, the sins of Ephraim are exposed and the crimes of Samaria revealed. They practise deceit, thieves break into houses, bandits rob in the streets; but they do not realise that I remember all their evil deeds. Their sins engulf them; they are always before me. They delight the king with their wickedness, the princes with their lies. They are all adulterers, burning like an oven whose fire the baker need not stir from the kneading of the dough till it rises. On the day of the festival of our king the princes become inflamed with wine, and he joins hands with the mockers. Their hearts are like an oven;

they approach him with intrigue. Their passion smoulders all night; in the morning it blazes like a flaming fire. All of them are hot as an oven; they devour their rulers. All their kings fall, and none of them calls on me.

Read it through again.

So what's God saying?

In this passage, God speaks of sins exposed, crimes revealed – deceit, robbery, adultery: 'they do not realise that I remember all their evil deeds'. Our sins are always before him – yes, *even* the ones we commit within the privacy of our Aztec Silver cocoons with airbags and electric windows. It's a well-known fact that many of us change into 'demons' when we get behind the wheel, muttering obscenities and conversing with rude hand signals, forgetting that God can see all this. I suppose that getting into a car is a bit like stepping into another world – we're in charge of our destiny (if we're driving, that is). The space inside my Prussian Blue saloon is *my* space, nobody else's. Perhaps we're gripped with a possessiveness, and a competitiveness. Plus we think we're hidden – after all, we can look out much more easily than people can look in. Just remember, though, that God doesn't need to peer through windows: he's inside the car with you! So God might be saying to you, 'Think car! Think ME!' Come on – come for a ride with me and Lil and I'll show you what I mean.

Well, before we can go anywhere we've got to wait until the car in front's parked. 'Come on, love, you could get a bus in there . . . she's making a right job of it . . .' THINK GOD – patience, am *I* the best parker in the world? No. Have I ever been glad of the patience of others? Yes. This driver is someone God loves – and who says it's a woman? OK, there was a bit of judging going on there. Does *he* need help? No, he's parked – now we can go, slowly and patiently, *without* revving.

We're coming up to a mini-roundabout now and find that nobody's moving; they're all waiting for someone else to go. Why is there such a difficulty at mini-roundabouts? They're like normal-sized roundabouts but smaller, that's all – the same rules apply! So why?! Why does everyone hesitate? Ahem, THINK GOD. He's seen your frustrated hand signals and your death stares towards the other drivers. Remember that he loves *them* just as he loves you. They're not harming you, they're just a little cautious, that's all – pray for them. Think God.

OK, this is nice, a very pleasant neighbourhood, keeping to the 30 mph limit. We're cruisin', eh Lil? Yeah! A quick look in the rear-view mirror . . . what the . . . he might as well be on my back seat! If there's one thing that gets on my wick it's drivers who sit on your tail pressurizing you to go faster. Well, I'm not moving that speedometer one strand of a clergyman's tassel, no way José. THINK GOD. Pray for that driver, that he might not come to any harm or cause anybody else to. As he (or she) aggressively overtakes (as now), continue to pray for that person without looking to your right to exchange glances, mobile blasphemies or finger signals. Let him go on his (or her) way.

YOU: I don't believe it – she just took a picture of you, Sister!

ME: Did she? That happens quite a lot actually. Many people seem fascinated when they see a nun driving. Perhaps they expect us to cry 'Beam me up, Scotty!' when we need to pop to Waitrose.

Right: we can put our foot down a little bit now. Look, Lil! A Doberman – grrr! Yeah, she's loving it! Oh no! Brakes! What is this person doing?! 40 mph in a 60 mph zone I think! Come on – this is actually dangerous! Dear oh dear. Ahem, THINK GOD! The person in front may be slow for a number of reasons – may be learning, may be nervous, may even have had an accident recently and so is being cautious. And he or she is loved by God. So we back off and allow space. If we can overtake safely then we will; until then we'll pray for that person.

Happily there were no further incidents and we arrive safely back home. Good – there's a parking space. Mmm – it's a bit tight. Reverse, turn, straighten up – oops, hit the kerb. Let's try that again – go forward, now reverse, turn, strai . . . oops, *up* the kerb.

(25 minutes later) Yes!!! We're in! You're impressed, I can tell. Just one last thing about 'Think car! Think God!' – if you decide to pray in the car, don't close your eyes.

ME: Right, best be off – I think Lil's smiling. We need to go and say our prayers – and a few 'sorrys'. We'll meet you next in front of the box for *The Jeremy Kyle Show*. Are you *all right*? You've gone as white as an altar cloth, and you're clutching the arm rest. Here: take this bag. It's one of Lil's, but she won't mind. I *do* sympathize – the standard of driving today is terrible. Take it easy, lemon queasy!

74

15

Go! God's up next on The Jeremy Kyle Show

☺ RELAX

Father God, this is life and you are here, yes, even in the middle of this show. Bring me your peace, bring me your love as I listen for your word. In Jesus' name. Amen.

☺ ABSORB

The Jeremy Kyle Show is on early so we plate up toasted bagels with scrambled egg, grab our first latte of the day and plonk down, delicately, in front of the telly as the intro music begins. It's not long before it breaks into shouting! Accusation! Tears! *Beep-beep*! Shifting of chairs. Get in the heavies! Lie-detector tests! Raking up the past! Pointing fingers! Laughter from the audience. 'You're nuffin' but a *beep-beep*!' Jeremy's shiny shoes, black socks and neat suits – nice shirt, no tie. 'Can we have a box of tissues, please?' Tattoos, ear-rings, talk of drugs, theft. Camera shot backstage. 'He's takin' advantage!' Unmarried mothers, booze, sleeping around. 'You're too good for him, girl!' Can't get a job. Down the pub. 'Be a responsible father!' She had a bad upbringing. Walking off stage. 'The relationship's over!' No trust any more. 'Where's Graham?'

He'll offer support. 'You'll get help, we promise.' 'She's a *beep* liar!' 'You've done *beep* nuffin' for 'im!' ASBO. Turning over a new leaf. 'It's over.' 'But I love 'im.' 'Look at me!' 'Stop swearing!' '*Beep-beep* no!'

YOU: Where's Lil?
ME: She's covered her ears and gone back to bed –
I don't blame her. Shall we hear what God wants
to say?

When we're ready, it's . . .

☞ BIBLE TIME

Let's read Numbers 15.37–41.

> The LORD said to Moses, 'Speak to the Israelites and say
> to them: "Throughout the generations to come you are
> to make tassels on the corners of your garments, with
> a blue cord on each tassel. You will have these tassels to
> look at and so you will remember all the commands of
> the LORD, that you may obey them and not prostitute
> yourselves by chasing after the lusts of your own hearts
> and eyes. Then you will remember to obey all my com-
> mands and will be consecrated to your God. I am the
> LORD your God, who brought you out of Egypt to be
> your God. I am the LORD your God."'

Read it through again.

So what's God saying?

The text that immediately jumps out at me is 'not prostitute
yourselves by chasing after the lusts of your own hearts and

eyes'. A lot of the issues and conflicts on *The Jeremy Kyle Show* centre around someone sleeping with somebody else when he or she shouldn't have, wanting to satisfy his or her own desires and not thinking about anyone or anything else. Many of the guests are single parents or children of single parents; some don't know their parents; some were put into care at an early age. These may be unfortunate victims of people who have done what they liked, chasing after the lusts of their own hearts and eyes, without giving much thought to the consequences. This won't be true in some cases but it will be in many. So as human beings, we can do what the hell we like, can't we? We don't need any 'commandments'. We don't need to obey anyone, do we? We can manage our lives perfectly well without the guidance of anyone else. Yeah, right. Perhaps God wants to help you in an area of your life where *you're* making the rules, not him?

Before I became a Sister, I enjoyed being part of our church choir. One night our practice was disturbed by a girl in her early teens – we'll call her Tia – who had come into the church with the clear intent of causing problems. We eventually asked her to leave. On my way out I came across Tia again leaning against the porch wall. 'Christianity's just loads o' rules, innit?' she asked. My response was an inadequate babble. So perhaps Tia would like to ask God that question – they're up next on *The Jeremy Kyle Show*.

JK: Backstage – the Father who desperately wants to
        be reconciled with his children. They say they don't
        know you, mate. You don't seem to have been a
        part of their lives. Why on earth would they want
        to know you?

GOD: I have always been there, closer than they think. Watching, waiting, loving them. They just haven't realized; they don't know about me.

JK: OK, not convinced. Do your own explaining because Tia's up on the show!

(music and applause as Tia enters)

TIA: You've never been in my *beep* life! You just wanna tell people what to *beep* do all the time! Thou shalt not do this, thou shalt not do that! Who the *beep* hell d'ya think you are?! My muvva left me ages ago, I loved 'er and one day she was, like, just gone! My bruvva don't care nuffin' about anythin' 'cept *beep* crack and gettin' laid! Dad's out most of the time wiv' his new bit; she 'ates my *beep* guts! I'm doin' *beep* at school 'cos I don't know nuffin'! The only mates I 'ave are out of their 'eads most of the time! The coppers'll do me if I get caught nickin' again! There's nuffin' to do round 'ere 'cept take the *beep* out of people and get *beep*! Yeah, I sleep around, 'cos I want to. What else am I gonna do? So I come to church one night an' what? A bunch of miserable *beep* do-gooders who turfed me out 'cos they were scared I'd upset their singin', which was *beep* anyway! You an' your people are a bunch of hypocrites who don't know nuffin' but pretend you know it all, that you're better than me, so just *beep* off!

GOD: I'm so pleased you're talking to me, Tia. Lots don't, or if they do they come to me as the person they think I'd like to see. You've come to me as you are. It's a good place for us to start talking.

JK: Well, this sounds like it could be a successful
reunion – can we have some tissues for Tia,
please? I wish you both well. Tia and her Father,
ladies and gentlemen!
(Tia exits to music and applause)

Tia was right in that Christianity has rules, but don't all good
parents provide their children with boundaries, with rules?
I'm certain Tia would have benefited from some. God guides
us through life by asking us to obey the Ten Commandments,
which can be summarized into the one commandment –
that we should love one another. If you, I and everyone else
followed God's advice here, there would be no *Jeremy Kyle
Show*, no drug addiction, no wars, no murders. Hang on!
Religion's been the cause of many wars! Yes – or should we
say *humankind*'s been the cause of these wars?

Would you like to say anything to God on *The Jeremy Kyle
Show*? Do you know the Ten Commandments? Do you try
to live life following God's advice? By the way, don't forget
the unwritten 'rules' of 'thou shalt *enjoy* God and his world'
and 'thou shalt *live*'! I'm not sure I see evidence of either on
The Jeremy Kyle Show.

ME: Lil? Lil! Come on, lazy girl. Jeremy's gone now.
She prefers David Dickinson; I think it's because
he wears a tie and has bouffant hair. Okey-dokey,
we'll catch you at the garden centre next where,
naturally, if we want to consult our Bible, we'll
have to sit down – in the café – which means we'll
have to buy something (like a cinnamon latte with
cream). See you later, hot potater; with my mutt,
crinkle cut!

16

Go! The garden centre – a most holy place?

———•✦•———

☺ RELAX

Jesus, this is life and you are here. Speak to all my senses, draw me to you, fill me with life, the life only you can give. Amen.

☉ ABSORB

Yay! Lil and I love garden centres! They speak to us of the great outdoors, leisure time, holidays, hobbies – they're kind of life-giving, aren't they? You might visit Tesco every week but a garden centre's more, well, spontaneous, isn't it? Smell that scent of natural wood as we breeze through the entrance – mmm! Lil's rubbing noses with a gnome. Windmills, birdbaths, welly-boot key rings, barbecues, garden clogs, fleeces and catfish pellets – it's all here. Uh-oh: Lil's pulling us past the wind chimes, garden giraffes, grow tunnels and Gelgem window clings to the pet department.

YOU: Clever. What do you think she's after?
ME: Well, I'd like to think it was popcorn chicken, but look: it's rabbit dung. Her equivalent of M&M's,

I suppose. She can have some beef cigars, and that's her lot.

We pass shelves of Gerty Guinea Pig's Complete Muesli to enter the book and novelty gift department. There's the Kitchen Garden Survival Kit. Greatest Granddad money boxes. Porky Pink Pig teapot cosies. Need a Hot Stone Massage Kit? Ah yes: *The Complete Idle Office Book*. Real-ale chutney. Cupcake pens. Malt-whisky marmalade. Bottoms-Up corkscrews. Novelty aprons. Oh: *The Cookie and Biscuit Bible* and *The Soup Bible* – mmm . . . lovely as they may be, I prefer this one (I pull out my NIV in a Filofax style). Got yours? Let's go grab a slab of carrot cake and a latte.

When we're ready, it's . . .

✐ BIBLE TIME

Let's read Hebrews 9.1–5.

> Now the first covenant had regulations for worship and also an earthly sanctuary. A tabernacle was set up. In its first room were the lampstand and the table with its consecrated bread; this was called the Holy Place. Behind the second curtain was a room called the Most Holy Place, which had the golden altar of incense and the gold-covered ark of the covenant. This ark contained the gold jar of manna, Aaron's staff that had budded, and the stone tablets of the covenant. Above the ark were the cherubim of the Glory, overshadowing the atonement cover. But we cannot discuss these things in detail now.

Read it through again.

So what's God saying?

There are lots of 'things' in this passage, aren't there? A tabernacle, lampstand, table, bread, curtains, the golden altar of incense, the ark of the covenant, the gold jar of manna, Aaron's staff, the stone tablets, the cherubim, the atonement cover – phew! There's lots of things in this garden centre too. So do you think God might want to say something about the things in our lives? Can a garden centre be a most holy place?! Yes, it can. I'll show you . . .

If we believe that God is the Maker of all things, then this garden centre is indeed a most holy place. Take 'Tickle Monster' egg cups. They're fun, and fun's an important element of life with Jesus – it feeds our soul. How about a 'Great British Baking Kit'? Marvellous. Baking's a loving thing to do for someone else; it's creative; it's therapeutic; and the results are, hopefully, nourishing – that's Godliness. Birdfeeding stations and birdwatcher's notebooks? Superb – looking after and studying God's creations. What could be better? Fancy a 'Mac in a Sac'? A reassuring little bundle that'll protect you in the unpredictable British climate – reassurance and protection speak of God. The garden centre: 'tis a most holy place indeed, but I feel duty bound to warn you that God could be forgotten quite easily and that I could spend £200 making a holy place for *myself*. How? Allow me to show you. Take a deep breath and limber up because . . . it's a nun on the run!

Yes!!! That rolling pin's just like the one Nigella uses – I could be in the same league as her if I buy it! Mmm . . . beetroot horseradish with a gingham lid cover – that'll impress Jan when she comes round next week! A gazebo! Yes! I could invite all my friends round; they'll think I'm really posh, just like one of those *Real Housewives of Atlanta*! Woohoo! Got to have a hanging basket, two perhaps – that'll *really* give the neighbours a new standard to aim for! Polka-dot measuring spoons! They'll look so good hanging up because I really am such a fun person to be around – I am, really! Ooh! Cherry Kiss home fragrance melters – I must have them, they're so *me*! Great! A canvas of a huge flower! See, I *am* fun! Better get one of an old man of the village next to a tractor, circa 1940, because I *am* interested in local history. Wayhay! It's Yankee Candles – *got* to have a couple of those! Hazelnut Coffee I think, because it smells of sophistication, and Pink Dragon Fruit to show my exotic-ness! Chintz-handled secateurs – I don't do any gardening but they'd look great propped up somewhere! Oh, and I must have that Lazy Sunday stripy ceramic toast rack, teapot and biscuit barrel set – I'd feel so much better in the mornings if I had those. Have I got enough left for that box of marbles – I need some fun – and that pack of Keep Calm and Carry On napkins? Yes, I have. Brilliant. I feel soooo good. Those things will really make me happy!

Phew! I nearly lost my veil doing that, you know. Now let's see. All those things may well make me happy for a little while, but the novelty wears off. Been there, done that, bought the T-shirt. I can assure you it won't be long before I'm back for another spree.

I bought some of those items because I wanted to be a certain person – fun, exotic, wealthy, like someone I've seen on telly perhaps. The 'things' made 'me'. In doing this, though, I'm selling my soul, I'm betraying the *real* me, the one God uniquely made. I'll never be happy unless I know who *I* am.

Pretending to be someone else is the cause of a whole polka-dot bucketful of problems.

I wanted to have, to possess, to prove I could afford to buy those things; to prove my wealth perhaps, my standing in society. Those 'things' became my security, they made me look good in front of other people, they made me acceptable.

In summary, those things became my gods. They would make my home a most holy place for me, but not for God. I'd forgotten about *him* completely. After all, I found all I was looking for in life in what I bought, didn't I? Well, in a word: No. Created things will never fully satisfy our souls – only the Creator can do that. God wants us to have quality of life in *him*, our security in *him* and our wealth in *him*. He's a jealous God. He demands that things take their proper order under *him*. Anything else is idolatry.

I drive my Sisters crazy because I'm a minimalist. There's not a lot in my cell. Perhaps I'm afraid of attaching myself to things and not to God. We need to grow a certain detachment from the created to the Creator. Once we do that we begin to see him in all things; 'things' suddenly begin to look different, have different values. They become triggers to God. We look through them to see the Giver of all good gifts – and there's plenty of those in here, so enjoy.

ME: Right, now Lil's finished her cigar, we're going to have some meditation time in the Yankee Candle department. We'll be propping up the bar in our next session. If you get there first, mine's a Coke – lemon, no ice. A still water and a packet of cheese and onion for Lil. Cheers!

17

Go! Mixing it in the Rose and Crown

———•·•·•———

☺ RELAX

God, this is life and you are here. You wanted to be where people were. Be with me in my heart, in my understanding. In Jesus' name. Amen.

☺ ABSORB

YOU: *(through clenched teeth you whisper)* I can't believe I'm walking into a pub with a nun. I think I've just been promoted to the board of Embarrassment & Sons Limited. Everyone's stopped talking. And look, there's a gang of mean-looking skinheads glaring our way.

ME: *(whispering)* Silly, that's my darts team. They're not happy I'm missing a match tonight – quarter-final too. Now calm down and get 'em in. Mine's a pint of Saturday Night Ferret. Off you go.

YOU: What?!!!

ME: Just kidding. Please may I have a Coke, and a still water and a packet of cheese and onion for Lil.

We perch cautiously on a couple of upholstered stools in as quiet an area as we can find. We seem to be yesterday's news already as the witty banter in the Rose and Crown resumes. I love that smell of beer, don't you? Reminds me of a warm summer evening. Friendly bar staff in black with spiky hair cruise past every now and again (they wouldn't look out of place in Costa). Lots of wood and brass. Chalkboards with menus and entertainment details. Guinness. The *chink-chink* of ice. Chunky chips. Tomato ketchup. Ladies chatting – a lone female could come in here and not feel intimidated, I think. Round tables scattered with glass-mats. From under the table we hear a *croarrrrk* – Lil's enjoyed her cheese and onion. Black and white pictures depicting ancient local scenes adorn the walls – grubby children play in a farmyard, and a blacksmith stands proudly next to his anvil in what's now a Ken's Fried Chicken. Floral curtains. More chips – and a lasagne, looks like. It's quite dark. Men's voices dominate. This table's sticky. A brass footrail surrounds the bar. Dartboard. Guinness bar-towels. Malibu. Pimm's. Black-handled optics. Hobgoblin, Bishop's Finger. Plump, chintzy cushions. A beamed ceiling. Dry-roasted peanuts. A brass bar-bell. Floorboards. A pool table. One fruit machine. Newspapers. Table numbers. Wall lamps create a relaxing ambience, albeit too dark to read a menu, so it's a good job we have backlit Kindles.

When we're ready, it's . . .

☞ BIBLE TIME

Let's read James 2.14–19 (as I was reading this passage a man approached me to talk about his faith – a 'God-incidence', I think).

What good is it, my brothers and sisters, if someone claims to have faith but has no deeds? Can such faith save them? Suppose a brother or a sister is without clothes and daily food. If one of you says to them, 'Go in peace; keep warm and well fed,' but does nothing about their physical needs, what good is it? In the same way, faith by itself, if it is not accompanied by action, is dead. But someone will say, 'You have faith; I have deeds.' Show me your faith without deeds, and I will show you my faith by my deeds. You believe that there is one God. Good! Even the demons believe that – and shudder.

Read it through again.

So what's God saying?

Faith and deeds go together like Posh and Becks. If we have faith in Jesus then this should bear fruit in what we do and how we do it. Imagine that skinhead over there were to have an accident with a dart. We would try to do what we could to help him, wouldn't we? We wouldn't just walk off saying, 'Hope you get better. All the best, mate', would we? You've gotta mix it, hombre. Perhaps God wants you to dwell on how you mix.

Have you ever mixed your drinks? I did once, in my youth. What resulted wasn't a pleasant experience. However, enough of that! Mixes in life are important. The key is getting your balance right, and that balance will be different for all of us. Snickers bars are OK as part of a healthy diet; a pint of Granny Wouldn't Like It is OK every now and again. So as part of a calorie-controlled Godly lifestyle, let's pick some mix to get you thinking.

Whatever your ministry is in your walk with Jesus (accountant, baker, insurance salesman, priest, flower arranger, cleaner), your 'fuel' comes from your time spent with God. If you don't look after your prayer life, your actions will suffer. Example: we have an online ministry using Facebook and Twitter. There is absolutely NO WAY we could work without replenishing our fuel, our spiritual life. I feel the difference when I don't spend enough time with God. I feel I'm running on empty. Prayer and action: mix it, baby.

All work and no play makes Lil a dull Jack. Lil enjoys listening to music (her fave composer's Bach). Her mind, body and spirit need chill-out time and stimulation for renewal, for recharging. We're the same. What do you enjoy doing – Zumba, playing Candy Crush Saga on your phone, knitting penguins, charting the history of cardboard-box development? Do you make time for it? Is work edging it out? If it is, to use the words of Del Boy Trotter, 'Don't be a plonker!' Do something about it, because it's important you have enough leisure time or play time. If you don't know what you enjoy doing, get in touch with your inner child and enjoy finding out! Now this next bit's significant: our God actually tells us to *have a day off each week*, a Sabbath day! That's because he made us and so knows what we need. Uh-oh: I can feel a Sabbath rap coming on . . .

> Listen up! *(boom-boom-bah, boom-ba-boom-bah)*
> Takin' note of God, restin' up your bod,
> Probs with a Sunday? Then duvet day on Monday
> Come on, man, get with it, followin' his Spirit,
> No need for an excuse, for holy hangin' loose. Diggit?

Work and play: if you dig it then mix it, honey.

How's your worship? All right? Take it or leave it? A bit boring? Samey? We're incredibly lucky in having a huge variety of worship styles out there. A friend of mine loved the traditional Anglican worship at her parish church, but every now and again would visit the Pentecostal church for a livelier worship experience, describing it as the icing on the cake. So if you feel like it, why not try a Messy Church? A Taizé-style evening prayer perhaps? Worship at a church of a different denomination? Occasionally treading on unfamiliar ground can often clear the air for God to speak quite powerfully. We can get stuck in a rut, albeit a comfortable one, and forget to expect the unexpected. Worship – no harm in mixing it, Fred.

Lastly: church and non-church. Becoming a Christian doesn't mean we begin hanging out with a holy crew and spend all our time in churches and charity shops – except if you're a nun. We may feel a bit uncomfortable with non-Christian friends when we're new to faith, but we shouldn't stop mixing. We're all made in the image of God. He can be seen in all people and he's everywhere, even in this pub. So every social mix can be holy – you can learn from others, they can learn from you. Church and non-church: mix it, amigo.

We'll each have a different mix of mixes – some of us will spend more time praying than playing, some of us will rest more than 'do'. So what's *your* mix?

ME: Right, I'd best mix it with the lads. I wonder how they're getting on. Uh-oh: there's tears; it doesn't look good. Oh, it's nothing to do with the darts: Mudslinger's just grieving for his beloved pair of

Doc Martens that've accidently been used as
flower pots by his youngest. See you next at Tesco's
café, the sausage-roll end of the counter. No,
Lil, you're not having a half of Wolf In Sheep's
Clothing. Good night!

18

Go! Every little helps –
helps us forget God?

☺ RELAX

Father God, this is life and you are here. Bring me to the haven of your love, bring me the love in your word. In Jesus' name. Amen.

☺ ABSORB

After feeling suitably embarrassed for not knowing how to work the 'make-your-own' hot-drinks machine, and consequently holding up a long queue, we make ourselves comfortable in Tesco's café – you have a tea and a decent-sized bowl of chips and I have a latte, of course. Cleopatra, the clapped-out Renault Clio, has been strategically parked so that we can wave to Lil, who's currently looking very funny, standing on the driver's seat with her front legs on the wheel. Indeed, a couple of passing children are pointing and giggling. Some screaming toddlers draw our attention back into the café. The *beep-beep-beep* of the checkouts provides constant background noise. Jostling trolleys. Some glum shoppers – usually men who just want to be somewhere else. The hum of chat. Nice comfy leather-effect seats.

'Economy-class' chairs are scraping the floor as post-shoppers arrive at their wood-effect tables with trays of tea, toasted teacakes, napkins and those little pods of milk that are fiddly to undo. Toblerone-shaped table menus promote free toast or fried bread, and free Wi-Fi. Deep-red walls and huge circular lightshades create a coffee-shop ambience – nearly. Two huge canvases – one of a red pepper; the other of a raspberry and an apple. Staff in dark-red shirts, navy trousers, aprons and pit caps, armed with J-cloths and anti-bac spray bustle past us as we reach for our Bibles.

When we're ready, it's . . .

☞ BIBLE TIME

Let's read Zechariah 1.1–6.

> In the eighth month of the second year of Darius, the word of the LORD came to the prophet Zechariah son of Berekiah, the son of Iddo: 'The LORD was very angry with your ancestors. Therefore tell the people: this is what the LORD Almighty says: "Return to me," declares the LORD Almighty, "and I will return to you," says the LORD Almighty. Do not be like your ancestors, to whom the earlier prophets proclaimed: this is what the LORD Almighty says: "Turn from your evil ways and your evil practices." But they would not listen or pay attention to me, declares the LORD. Where are your ancestors now? And the prophets, do they live for ever? But did not my words and my decrees, which I commanded my servants the prophets, overtake your ancestors? Then they repented and said, "The LORD

Almighty has done to us what our ways and practices deserve, just as he determined to do."'

Read it through again.

So what's God saying?

This passage is telling us that the people and their ancestors had turned away from God to live life their own way. Zechariah is passing on a message from God – 'Return to me'. They'd forgotten about him. Could God be saying the same to you now? I enjoy coming to Tesco but it can play a little part in helping us forget God. How? Because it's so good at satisfying our needs, as we can discover quite easily in the café . . .

It's time to go into 'whisper and shifty-eye mode' because we're going to be nosey and take a peek at what our fellow chip-eaters have bought here in Tesco. How have *their* needs been satisfied? So what do you see? A computer mouse and keyboard? Great. Cycle lights – that'll keep him safe on the road. A tub of Utterly Butterly, lovely to start the day with. A Special Edition Frijj milkshake – now you're talking: these really are *the* bizz. Socks. Flowers – those'll brighten up the living room. Look: they've just had their photos developed. That girl's just raced from the pharmacy and is hurrying to stick an anti-hay fever spray up one nostril. Oh, listen: this couple have just booked their holiday to France! Mega – so exciting. She's also bought a lovely card for Mike and Diana's anniversary – nice. They're so chuffed they even managed to get their Euros here – hadn't realized they could do that. That youngish bloke at 10 o'clock's bagged a couple of low-energy light bulbs – must be an eco-friendly BOGOF. Hey: that lady over there's just picked up her dry cleaning – I had no idea Tesco did that. Hang on: must just check Lil – yep, she's OK, she's busy watching the carwash gang. Fancy that: while you're shopping in here your car's being shampooed – so convenient. The man next to us is checking car-insurance documents – Tesco car insurance; you can get that sorted here too. Crumbs, look over there: he's got a mini flatscreen telly and a mobile phone in his trolley. Yes, that dress does suit you, love; perfect for Saturday. And those neon wristbands will look so good at the gym. What about this last person? Mmm – crumpets, yes, and a huge bar of Dairy Milk, ideal for a night in. Right, I think we've done enough; we can return to 'normal mode' now. Looks like you can get pretty much everything from this place – a real one-stop shop. Wonderful. I enjoy coming to Tesco. It's not just the produce, there's a social vibe too, isn't there? You can meet up with friends over a courgette, clash trolleys with someone you've never even met, put the world to rights with Aggie on the checkout and check your emails over a Classic Big Breakfast. Yes, Tesco really *can* satisfy our every need, can't it?

Yes, admittedly, Tesco and other superstore chains can tick a lot of boxes, but not all of them, Pedro. Don't forget God and what *he* can give you. He's the only one who can give you real soul food, and your soul is where 'you' begin – get that right and the rest comes right too. So let's check out what *isn't* on the shelves.

Peace. No, not the Bird's Eye frozen variety – PEACE. St Augustine famously said that our hearts would be restless until they'd found their rest in God. A drift around the aisles can be so tranquil – at midnight – but can't compare with the tranquillity of being in a relationship with your Maker.

When your soul discovers its Creator it kind of settles down. It's found its origin, its roots, there's no need to search any further, job done, 'nuff said. We cease rushing after the latest fad that promises so many things. We're given the deepest peace that helps us in all areas of our lives, in the joys and in the sadnesses. You can't buy *that* from Tesco Direct.

Joy. No, not the lady behind the fish counter – JOY. Knowing God and experiencing relationship with him is truly awesome. A tub of Ben & Jerry's can give us joy, but nothing like this. We're talking *deep joy* that warms you inside and lasts. Even when tragedy strikes it remains. It doesn't mean a permanent smile like Ronald McDonald, but a deep happiness inside that comes from getting with God. You can't get *that* from Tesco's Finest.

Hope. No, no, not the album by Hillsong – HOPE. Jesus' life, death and resurrection are the only things that give me hope. His miracles tell me that in every situation he is there to help, to answer prayer. His death for me, you and everyone else tells me to trust him. His resurrection tells me that everything will work out. In everything I have hope. You can't get *that* with your Clubcard.

Love. No, no, no, not Tesco's body spray for women – LOVE. Knowing that he who made you loves you just as you are – even if you'd rather scoff a Pot Noodle on Sunday morning than go to church – is probably *the* most amazing thing to discover. God, the Maker of everything, loves *me*?! Yes, you! But I use DIY checkouts because I don't like people, and steal parking spaces reserved for families. God may not like some of your ways but he loves you all the same and wants to help you grow and live life to the max. Now you can't get any of *that* at the deli, Kelly.

All this, along with fulfilment, adventure, the ability to cope with life's ups and downs and more, are the fruits of a life with God. There are no BOGOFs either: it's a job lot; your trolley will be full, and for eternity too – *that* beats 24-hour opening.

ME: That was a decent latte. Hope you enjoyed your chips. Lil's now entertaining a growing crowd of kiddies with her 'Dance Like An Egyptian' moves. You know I've often wondered where she came from. We're at the car boot next, in the leisure-food area. See you around, with my hound!

19

Go! Trusting God at the car boot

☺ RELAX

Jesus, this is life and you are here. As I walk, as I sit, as I stand, move me with your sacred word. Amen.

☺ ABSORB

The heady smell of leisure food infiltrates our nostrils as we meet by the Shake, Cattle 'n' Coal barbecue and refreshment area. It's car boot time! We limbo under the tape barriers and I have to start keeping an eye on Lil – do you know she actually nicked the meat from someone's sandwich once? There's country and western music playing. Leopard-skin mini-skirts are being sold en masse from the back of a Mazda. Replica Laliques going for a song. Gaudy Clarice Cliff looky-likees are being offered at £1.50. Stacks of Smashey & Nicey videos. Babygrows (shan't be needing any of those). A Raleigh Boxer. A complete fireplace. Picture frames. Ornaments galore. Cycle cranks. A tartan shopping trolley. A 1970 *Guinness Book of Records*. Passing pushchairs bulge with jigsaws and brooms (where are the children?). Dealers quietly snap up bargains while enjoying a ciggie. A ship's wheel. Hang on: a ship's wheel?! Newly arrived husbands leave their wives to travel the circuit while they head off for a home-made scone. An elderly lady's haggling over a £2 fleece jacket. Dogs yawn, yelp when trodden on, and even the most introverted can't wait to meet another canine for a bit of stimulation. *Now That's What I Call Music* tapes from 1983. Now this is what I call the right time to take the next exit and see what God might want to say in all this.

When we're ready, it's . . .

✐ BIBLE TIME

Let's read Joshua 6.1–7.

> Now the gates of Jericho were securely barred because of the Israelites. No one went out and no one came in. Then the LORD said to Joshua, 'See, I have delivered Jericho into your hands, along with its king and its fighting men. March round the city once with all the armed men. Do this for six days. Make seven priests carry trumpets of rams' horns in front of the ark. On the seventh day, march round the city seven times, with the priests blowing the trumpets. When you hear them sound a long blast on the trumpets, make the whole army give a loud shout; then the wall of the city will collapse and the army will go up, everyone straight in.' So Joshua son of Nun called the priests and said to them, 'Take up the ark of the covenant of the LORD and make seven priests carry trumpets in front of it.' And he ordered the army, 'Advance! March round the city, with an armed guard going ahead of the ark of the LORD.'

Read it through again.

So what's God saying?

I think God's saying, 'Trust me.' Don't you think the trust the Israelites had in God was pretty amazing? The gates of Jericho were secure, no entry, no way José. However, God told Joshua that the city was theirs. They just needed to march around the city 13 times over seven days, blow their trumpets, shout and then simply watch the walls come down. I wonder if any of them thought, 'Really?' They did what God asked them to do and, hey presto, Jericho was theirs. They trusted God. Do you?

We can be a bit like the Israelites, traipsing around this car boot, round and round, searching for a bargain. There's a certain amount of trust here too, isn't there? Do we trust that our new Philips CD player actually works? It had better – it cost three quid. What about these CDs? 'They haven't fallen off the back of a lorry, have they?' 'If my bedside lamp with bejewelled tartan shade doesn't work, you will be here next week, won't you?' 'I can't get that fireplace in my Smart car – oh, you can deliver, can you? Yes, I'll pay up front.' Mmm . . . trust. We may not trust everyone we meet. Unfortunately, many of us learn that from an early age, but how do we feel about trusting God? What if *he* had a stall at this car boot? Would we trust what he has to offer? Let's see. 'Lil, will you leave that little girl's hot dog alone!'

OK, here we are at God's stall. No car boot here? No need, I suppose. There seem to be lots of people walking up to this stall then scurrying away. They're not stopping. Many are peering from afar, behind the 'out-of-date but eatable' snack bar. Let's see what God's offering – 'FORGIVENESS', 'LOVE AND RELATIONSHIP', 'ETERNAL

LIFE'. Well, it's certainly different! Let's listen to what people are saying:

GORDON: Come on, Steph – I don't need to be forgiven; it's a load of old tosh.

STEPH: Yeah, you're prob'ly right, Gord. God wouldn't love me anyway; I've done too much.

GORDON: Oh you 'ave, 'ave yer?

Yes, he would love you, Steph! He's come for people like you and me! He's always loved us, always been there, but we haven't known it! Come back! OK, what about Stan, Stan the Burger Man:

STAN: Eternal life? We die and that's it. THIS is our life NOW. Eternal life? I may as well go the whole hog and believe in aliens!

We can't prove it to you, mate. But, from our relationship with Jesus, we trust and believe in what he's promised us. There's loads of stories about saints helping people from beyond the grave. How can they help if they're dead? Right, here's someone else – looks like Bric-a-Brac Jack:

JACK: I can't believe anyone could forgive me for what I've done. I can't even say it out loud, I'm so ashamed. I'd like to think forgiveness was true . . .

It *is* true! We've all done things we're ashamed of – big things, little things. That's because we're *human*. When we're sorry, we can talk to God about it and ask him to help us change our ways. He forgives, removing any burden of guilt from us so that we can move on and freely live. Go on: take his FORGIVENESS! Hey, look, wow: he *is*! He's picking up the box marked FORGIVENESS. The other boxes are pushed his way too!

JACK: What? You want me to take ETERNAL LIFE and LOVE AND RELATIONSHIP too? I can't possibly afford all of them. How much are they, then?

There's no BOGOF offers here, fella. You take one, you automatically get the bundle. You want to know the cost? Just follow the Stallholder. He's following – and he's crying. He's soon going to be free of all that guilt that's trapped him up like that birdcage over there.

So how's *your* trust in God? Trusting usually comes as our relationship with him gets stronger, though even the most experienced Christians have lapses of trust. Trust builds in us as we read about God in the Bible, as we hear our friends' stories of their experiences with God, when he answers prayers, as we read about the lives of famous Christians and as we open ourselves up to him.

Know that he forgives you every time you tell him you're sorry. *Trust* him. Know that he loves you and wants a relationship with you – that's why Jesus came. *Trust* him. Know that you will live on after you've died. *Trust* him. Place yourself in his hands, just as the Israelites did.

ME: OK, Lil and I are off to get some leisure food. Do you realize that our next meeting will be our last? Can you believe it? We can't. Lil's distraught – she wouldn't even watch David Dickinson on the telly yesterday. So see you at the convent. Until then: if you come across any cheap candles . . .

20

Go! Wot no God – at the convent?!

☺ RELAX

Lord God, this is life and you are here. In this stillness may I hear your voice; in this quietness may I feel your love. Amen.

☺ ABSORB

The convent. Peace. Quiet. Stillness. We're lounging in comfy brown armchairs in a light, airy conservatory surrounded by low shelving chock-full of books. The cream venetian blinds sway in the light breeze. A wood pigeon warbles outside. Lil's on her belly on the mint-green carpet, her hind legs arranged like a frog's. She's dreaming, a pleasant one, I hope – probably chasing nuns who are wearing habits and veils made of Pedigree Chum. Deformed home-made patterned cushions adorn some of the armchairs; they haven't been plumped up since they embraced their last customer. The distant *clink* of coffee mugs. It's warm; sunlight speckles the room. There's a faint whiff of incense. An arum lily's attempting to reveal its beauty; a Christmas cactus awaits its turn.

YOU: Where *is* everyone?

ME: We disappear into the woodwork at regular
       intervals and then come out to pray. No – actually,
       everyone's doing something, somewhere, in silence.

A clock ticks. The hum of distant traffic. A door's opening
somewhere in the house. The creak of a floorboard. A door
closes. We hear a cough. Lil's woken from her sweet slumber
and is gnawing a dog biscuit, *craah, craaah*. A clock bongs
2 o'clock. Aah – we could easily drop off here. You lean back
in your armchair and stretch out your legs . . .

YOU: Sister, what's Lil doing? She's sitting stock still in
       front of that candle. You're not going to tell me
       she's praying?

ME: Oh yes, she's praying all right. She's trying to
       discern her vocation – she thinks it's to the
       priesthood. Well, the clues *are* there – she's a
       Parsons Jack Russell; she's used to a dog collar;
       she likes milky tea.

When we're ready, it's . . .

✎ BIBLE TIME

Let's read Isaiah 59.9–11.

> So justice is far from us, and righteousness does not reach
> us. We look for light, but all is darkness; for brightness,
> but we walk in deep shadows. Like the blind we grope
> along the wall, feeling our way like people without eyes.
> At midday we stumble as if it were twilight; among the
> strong, we are like the dead. We all growl like bears; we

moan mournfully like doves. We look for justice, but find none; for deliverance, but it is far away.

Read it through again.

So what's God saying?

Gosh, what a shocker of a passage! Check out these words:

So justice is far from us . . . righteousness does not reach us . . . all is darkness . . . we walk in deep shadows . . . we grope along the wall . . . like people without eyes . . . we stumble . . . we are like the dead . . . we growl . . . we moan . . . we look . . . but find none . . . it is far away.

Here I'm seeing God as 'justice' and 'righteousness', so it seems as though he's saying, 'There'll be times when you'll think I'm absent from you. You'll grope around looking for me but won't find me. You'll growl and moan because I don't seem to be there.' Have you ever felt that God's done a runner, that he's left you? I tell you, it's as painful as a seed in your dentures.

As nuns, do we experience God's apparent absence? Yes. Hang on a minute: how can you feel God's not around in a place teeming with nuns, priests, icons, holy water, crucifixes, Bibles and rosary beads?! I mean, it's like complaining you can't see the supernatural at Hogwarts, isn't it? Well, it's quite easy, because all those signs may point towards God but they're simply not *him*. They've been created but they're not *the* Creator our souls long for.

What's the absence of God feel like? Bad. Of course, you're the only one who can't sense him. Everyone else seems to be having a ball and smiling from ear to ear just to reinforce the point that they've got him and you haven't. Grrr – see how I'm growling like a bear? Lil likes it when I do that. The Bible's about as attractive as a ladder in your tights. And worship? It's a drag. He's not there; this whole thing was just one big illusion; Ricky Gervais was right. Humph!

So what do we do in these situations? Well, normally the first thing you have to do is to listen to annoying Christians telling you, 'God *is* there, you'll see'. As irksome as they may be, they do have a point. Think. How do you feel? Glum. That's because you're missing him. That means he *was* around you once, right? So when these times of despair crop up, always think back to how good things *have* been. Remember and rejoice in the closeness you've experienced with God. Then take heart. He *is* still there but perhaps he's not making it so obvious. He's acting like a parent letting his toddler walk on their own. This means you're in a stage of growth, although it may not feel that way. He wouldn't have led you to this stage if you weren't ready – take heart from that.

You've loved the joys, the peace, the love you've felt from him – but he's more than that. He doesn't want you to rely on what he gives you, he wants you to know him and to depend on him at a deeper level that goes beyond surface feelings. Once again, you're growing. Take heart.

God's bigger than you think. He often plays hide-and-seek with us, wanting us to see him in different ways and places, encouraging us to expand our view of him, which has become far too small. If you feel God's hiding from you, think. Do you go to church once a week and then forget him? Do you stick to the same devotions and prayers day in, day out? Then try something new. He's stretching you; you're being encouraged to grow, so take heart.

Don't do what I've done in the past when I've moaned like a dove because God hasn't appeared to be around. I've tended to go off in a sulk, not wanting to be around others who clearly don't struggle like I do (when in reality they do). However hard it may be, don't stop being around people. You'll need other Christians to help you through – they may actually be 'windows' to seeing God in new ways. Sit your bum firmly on a pew and ask him to show himself, then be open to whatever may present itself. Be prepared to be surprised, to encounter something new.

It had never occurred to me before, but God never seems absent now. He's shown me he's in all things, in all people, in all places. I couldn't get away from him if I tried! Lil and I don't want to anyway. I don't enjoy daily ecstasies or collapse every week from being slain in the Spirit; it's enough to know he's there and that we're in relationship.

So if you ever feel God's absent, by all means stumble, grope, growl and moan, but take heart – you're growing.

ME: Right – we're off. Oh, hang on: this is the convent; we can't go. So we'll see you next at the . . . Oh, this has been, um, our last, um, session . . . our *last* one, our *very* last one. There *isn't* a next time; this is *it*. Lil, come here – don't cry; you'll start me off. Oh, you *have* started me off (*sniff, sniff*)! Oh dear . . . (*sniff*), can you fetch (*sniff*), that box of tissues. That's it (*sniff*), give one to Lil . . . Oh, we need to pray . . . *(The three of us sit around a cream pillar-candle holding hands and paws, watching the bobbing flame.)*

Light of the world, we thank you for our time together; for the blessings of friendship, for your gift of humour, for the Holy Bible, for your living word.

We thank you for being our God, for the joy of seeing you in all things, in all people and in all places. We thank you for your Son and for your Holy Spirit. Bless each of us as we journey on. In Jesus' name. Amen.

YOU: Amen.

LIL: *Crooooaarrrck.*

YOU: I've been thinking – there is one place we *could* go next. How about the gym?

ME: The GYM?! When I said the Bible should be read everywhere, I meant . . . I *meant* . . . OK, everywhere: you win. Let's go to 'Tussle with the Muscle' with my Jack Russell. She'll love the treadmill but the machines aren't exactly habit-friendly, are they? And if I hear anyone say, 'We'll have nun of that in here', I'll . . .